For As Long As I Can

A Son's Memoir of His Father's Dying Request

Roland E. Cavanaugh

Betty Jo —
Blessings on you —
Roland E. Cavanaugh
Rev. 21:1-4

xulon PRESS

A portion of the net proceeds from the sale of this book will be donated to Hospice.

The cover photo was taken in 1993 off the coast of Greece.

The author welcomes your comments about this work. You can send a message to him at falaic@highstream.net

www.xulonpress.com

To Sammy,
David,
Carol and
Scott

Daddy was proud of every one of us. He told me so himself.

When he left us, it was as if a great tree had fallen in the forest, and left a lonesome place against the sky.

—Anonymous

A Preface

This journal is a labor of love. As Daddy said, "Hopefully, someone will find it interesting someday." It is of immense interest to me and will continue to be so for as long as I live in this world.

The basic thoughts here recorded were put to paper, by my own hand, in a leather journal that I began keeping from the first day that my father entered the hospital in High Point, North Carolina. That journal is one of the single most cherished possessions that I have at this time, a gift from God and my father. Sometimes I would simply remember the events as they happened. Other times, I would make a recording on my cell phone using the voice memo feature, or I would use a personal recorder. Some were written down on everything from the back of an envelope (from the many, many cards he received while in High Point) to a napkin that came with his latest meal.

His saying, "You might want to write this down," or "This probably ought to go into that 'book' you are writing," sometimes prefaced the stories I have recorded. (He always referred to it as a book, not a journal. He seemed to feel that it was more than I intended it to be, that is, simply a record of the last days of my father's earthly life.) It is a record that includes details of his daily life and activities, stories that were relative to our family's history or future, or simply items that he thought were interesting to share. While some of it tends to be redundant, hence the life of the terminally ill, it records accurately all that happened during the time he was with us.

It is the single best record that we have of our father's last days, conversations, struggles and hopes. I offer it in loving memory of him, knowing that we will one day meet again.

The nature of this narrative is by pretense subjective. It includes my personal thoughts, observations and interpretations of the events that are described. I have also included my thoughts as I have struggled to come to grips with his death. Those thoughts, especially, are not easy for me to share, but I trust that you will find them helpful or at least informative.

Journaling, in my opinion, is one of the purist forms of expression. In order to maintain that unique flavor, I have purposefully left most of the details in place. My desire is to present the account in its original form, largely untouched, except for grammatical, spelling and punctuation corrections. I trust that the inclusion of those everyday details makes my father's story both more personal and meaningful.

While this is a story that is painful for me to tell, it is one that I must share. If he thought it would help someone else going through similar struggles, I feel confident that Daddy would want it told as well. Although I have attempted to guard our family's privacy, certain elements shared are so germane to the story that they must be included. However, I have changed some names of people, and deliberately not given last names in some instances, all in the interest of privacy.

Finally, I must say that what began as a simple desire to record a "few thoughts" relative to my father's stay in High Point for physical rehabilitation soon became an obsession with me as we came to realize that his stay here would probably be the last of his earthly days. God has done all things well. While the words may bring tears, I hope that the humor also comes through, as well as the heart of our father, a heart that I really only got to know fully during the last weeks of his life. I am eternally grateful for our father's contribution to this material, both in action and spoken word.

While I present it to you humbly and with tremendous gratitude to God for His grace on my father and all of the family, let me share what came to be one of Daddy's favorite quotes, something John Wesley said on his deathbed, "But the best of all is, God is with us."

The following words from Shakespeare help give meaning as to why I ultimately became compelled to record so many of the experiences that I relate: "Give sorrow words; the grief that does not speak, knits up the o'er fraught heart and bids it break."

While the following words were recorded with tears, the process of putting pen to paper truly allowed my grief to speak. My prayer is that these words will speak to you as well.

Roland E. Cavanaugh
High Point, North Carolina
September 1, 2005

CONTENTS

Acknowledgements ....*xvii*

Introduction ....*xix*

ACT 1
NOVEMBER
SETTING THE STAGE **29**

Chapter 1   Sunday, November 28   *It Begins* 31

Chapter 2   Monday, November 29   *Suspicions* 33

Chapter 3   Tuesday, November 30   *Uncertainty* 35

ACT 2
DECEMBER
ADJUSTING THE SCRIPT **39**

Chapter 4   Wednesday, December 1   *God is With Us* 41

Chapter 5   Friday, December 3   *The Procedures Begin* 45

Chapter 6   Saturday, December 4   *One of the Hardest Things*..........................47

Chapter 7   Sunday, December 5   *A Gift from God*...........53

Chapter 8   Tuesday, December 7   *Rollercoaster Ride*........57

Chapter 9   Wednesday, December 8   *Running on Both Arms*............................63

Chapter 10   Thursday, December 9   *The Results Are In*........67

Chapter 11   Friday, December 10   *Final Plans*...................73

Chapter 12   Saturday, December 11   *Signed, Sealed and Delivered*......................77

Chapter 13   Sunday, December 12   *Investigating Options*...83

Chapter 14   Monday, December 13   *Potential Fallout*...........87

Chapter 15   Tuesday, December 14   *A Rough Month*.............91

Chapter 16   Wednesday, December 15   *Back (Nursing) Home Again*............................97

Chapter 17   Thursday, December 16   *Discretionary Funds*..101

Chapter 18   Friday, December 17   *I Remember It to This Day*...........................107

Chapter 19   Saturday, December 18   *Slowly Losing Control*......................111

Chapter 20   Sunday, December 19   *The Most Blessed Man on Earth*....................129

Chapter 21   Monday, December 20   *Two Major Issues*.......135

Chapter 22   Tuesday, December 21   *When I Get Out of Here*............................141

Chapter 23   Wednesday, December 22 *A Ton of Bricks* 147

Chapter 24   Thursday, December 23 *The Beginning of
                                     Letting Go* 155

Chapter 25   Friday, December 24   *More Than Clouds* 161

Chapter 26   Saturday, December 25 *A Faraway Look* 167

Chapter 27   Sunday, December 26   *Breaking the Spell* 171

Chapter 28   Monday, December 27   *I Could Stay Here All
                                     Night* 173

Chapter 29   Tuesday, December 28   *Lake Wobegon Days* ... 179

Chapter 30   Wednesday, December 29 *Contentment and
                                     Distress* 187

Chapter 31   Thursday, December 30 *God Has Worked
                                     Everything Out* 193

Chapter 32   Friday, December 31   *A Spiritual Butterfly* ... 197

ACT 3
JANUARY
CLOSING THE SCENE **203**

Chapter 33   Saturday, January 1   *See You Soon* 205

Chapter 34   Sunday, January 2   *Trying to Die* 209

Chapter 35   Monday, January 3   *The Good Eye Cries* ... 217

Chapter 36   Tuesday, January 4   *A Life in Pictures* 235

Chapter 37   Wednesday, January 5   *Sharing Stories* 237

Chapter 38   Thursday, January 6   *I Have Never Felt Like I Do Today* 247

Chapter 39   Saturday, January 15   *A Time for Everything* 263

Chapter 40   Tuesday, January 25   *How Long Will I Count the Days?* 271

ACT 4
FEBRUARY
WRITING A NEW STORY **273**

Chapter 41   Wednesday, February 2   *Further Down the Road* 275

Chapter 42   Friday, February 18   *I Love the Sun* 277

Chapter 43   Monday, February 21   *A Familiar Lump* 281

Chapter 44   Sunday, February 27   *He Was Walking* 283

ACT 5
EPILOGUE
HOPE SPRINGS ETERNAL **287**

When the Crabapple Blooms 293

Funeral and Graveside Scriptures 297

Recommended Resources 301

Acknowledgements

It is always hard to know where to begin when I think of all of the people that touched my father...

I must thank the staff at *Westchester Manor* nursing home. Their care, especially the weekend staff, was exemplary. We were very comfortable leaving him with you.

I also wish to say (once again!) thank you to the staff of 7 North at *High Point Regional Hospital*. As the plaque states, "He was so comfortable during his time here."

To the staff and congregation of *First Wesleyan Church*: words are not adequate to describe my thankfulness to God for your support and encouragement.

Hospice has always held a special place in my heart; that place has grown deeper through this experience.

It is impossible to thank all of the family and friends who came from near and far to offer an encouraging word to him.

I thank Cindy for allowing me all of those hours to be with him, to write...and to grieve. She has been by my side constantly.

Most importantly, I wish to thank God. He knew decades, even centuries ago, that Daddy and I would come together in High Point during that critical time in his life. May His Name be praised. He *has* done all things well.

The following people read the final draft and gave critical editing assistance:

Brad Meadows, BA in English, UNCG; Carroll Meadows, 30 years of public education, including administration and teaching English; and Linda Meadows, 30 years of teaching in public school.

Your objective comments and suggestions were very helpful. I sincerely appreciate your interest in reading the manuscript.

Also, Pastor Inthava Inthisane's help with scanning and getting the photographs ready to "go to press" was immeasurable; "Sabaidee."

I wish to sincerely thank my sister and brothers for providing many of the photographs used in this work. *This is our story.*

Finally, my father must also be thanked. His willingness for me to share his story and vulnerability are at the heart of this book. For without that final gift of generosity, there would be no story to tell. I have sensed his presence throughout this process.

Introduction

S amuel MacDonald Cavanaugh was born on October 21, 1927 to Roland Oscar and Vada Hanchey Cavanaugh in Duplin County, North Carolina. He grew up there, in the southeastern part of the state, about forty miles north of Wilmington. He actually came of age in the part of the county known by the locals as the "Northeast" community, seven miles east of Wallace and Rose Hill.

He was one of six children, having three older brothers, Charles, R. C., and Frank, and two sisters, Ruby, who resides in Virginia, and Sissie, who lives in the Fayetteville, North Carolina area. He was preceded in death by all of his brothers. He grew up on a farm, his father doing some farming, as well as operating a local sawmill.

He graduated second in his class from the *University of North Carolina School of Pharmacy* in 1949 and worked as a pharmacist for over 54 years. He worked in Wallace, Rose Hill, Whiteville and ultimately, Lumberton, NC. He owned a store in Rose Hill until 1972. He eventually settled in Lumberton and opened another store there that is still in operation today, "*Sam's Drug Store.*"

He was married to the former Elizabeth Rich until their divorce in the mid 1960s. Their union produced four children: Sammy, David, Carol and Roland. Sammy, a dental technician, and his wife Sandra live in Duplin County. They have two grown children, Vada and Austin. Austin is the first of our father's descendents to attend

UNC-Chapel Hill. He is just beginning his studies for dentistry; Daddy would be very proud. David lives in Lumberton with his wife Lynda. He worked with our father for 14 years at the drug store there, helping run the business; he continues to do so today. Carol lives in Duplin County with her husband Mike. They have three grown children, Eric, Ashly and Jason. Ashly earned her Pharm.D. degree from Campbell University in 2002, and carries on the lineage of registered pharmacists for our family.

I, Roland, am married to Cindy. We have been in ministry since 1988. I presently serve as Pastor of Congregational Care and Senior Adults at First Wesleyan Church in High Point, NC, having been there since 2001. I also direct our church's chaplaincy program. We visit the area hospitals each day, as well as the residents at our affiliate ministries, which include a 129-bed nursing home, a 69-bed assisted living facility and various forms of senior adult housing. High Point is nestled in the Piedmont region of North Carolina and is known as the "Furniture Capital of the World." It is a beautiful city, three hours from David and the drug store. It is even further from the other children.

Cindy and I, of course, call High Point home. For point of reference, our church is comprised of two campuses, four miles apart. The main campus is home of *First Wesleyan Church* and our state-of-the-art conference center, *Providence Place*. The nursing home, called *Westchester Manor*, is on the *Providence Place* campus and was opened in 2003. It was relocated from the Centennial St. campus. The Centennial St. campus includes an assisted living facility and senior adult housing units. That campus is also the home of *Grout Chapel*, where I conduct a worship service for senior adults each Sunday morning.

After his divorce from our mother, Daddy remarried in the late 1960s. (Our mother presently lives in Duplin County with her third husband, Ronald. At the time of this writing, he is undergoing chemotherapy treatments for Multiple Myeloma, a form of leukemia. She has one son by her second husband; his name is Delwood. He lives near Wallace with his wife Beverly and their young daughter. Delwood's father Hoover, with whom I lived from the age of 10 until I left home for college, died in 1982. Hoover treated me as if I was his own flesh, even telling others that I was his son, just like Delwood.)

Daddy's marriage to the former Barbara Colloms, who is from Tennessee, produced another son, Scott. Scott lives in eastern Tennessee with Kelly, his wife. They are raising two young boys, Collin and Ethan, at this time. Scott and Kelly both serve in the medical profession as nurses. His expertise and insight proved invaluable during our father's illness.

After a second divorce in the 1970s, our father never married again. Barbara currently lives in eastern Tennessee, maintaining close contact with Scott and other members of her family. (Scott actually returned to Tennessee with her when he was two years old. He has lived there ever since.)

Our father was active in many civic organizations over the years. He was directly involved with the *Duplin Times* newspaper and had a long relationship with *Alcoholics Anonymous* (A. A.). One of his most remarkable gifts was the ability to help others in need, especially those fighting alcohol and/or drug addiction. The list of persons he helped to win the battle over them will never be fully known. His personal battles no doubt gave him insight and a heart that few can ever understand.

His love of the pharmacy profession and service to people in general will long be remembered. He often stated that he had no real plans to retire. True to character, he managed to work up until the last eight weeks of his life.

He also loved to travel. In the latter years of his life, he was privileged to travel to several European countries including Greece, England, Scotland, Italy, Germany, Spain and France. Some of these he visited more than once.

His life is one that was full, yet not perfect. None of us are perfect, however, and we make our mistakes as we travel this journey called "life." During the last weeks of his life, the person that so many knew in the communities in which he served came forth. He was able to touch many people, and made friends at both the hospital and the nursing facility where he lived out his final days. While his life, like all of our lives, was filled with trouble and hardship, he always saw the good in people. Even when he was struggling himself, he was always eager to lend a helping hand to someone less fortunate. He was the full embodiment of the "old school" pharmacist, knowing the names of all of his customers, even recognizing their children. He would come from behind the counter to chat or to ask how you were doing. He always placed the concerns of others before his own, at times neglecting his personal welfare. While some may question the wisdom of this, there are certainly elements of this type of lifestyle that we would all do well to emulate.

At home alone, he fell on an early November day. He had actually fallen and broken his leg several months earlier in the spring. Since that time, however, he had used a wheelchair and walker and continued to go to work at the drug store. David picked him up in the morning and took him home in the evening several days each week...until November.

A direct result of the fall in November was his hospitalization in Lumberton. It was during the two weeks he was there that he lost the ability to walk. Thinking that physical therapy was in order, he entered *Westchester Manor* nursing facility for rehabilitation. This record tells the story of his time in High Point with me. All of his children rallied around him during his stay there. After two weeks in the facility, he developed pneumonia and entered *High Point Regional Hospital*. It was during his two-week stay in the hospital that he found out he had cancer. This journal actually begins with the day that he went to the hospital from the nursing home.

As the pain of his death recedes further into memory, the fruit of his life continues to come more sharply into focus. Only God really knows the people that he ultimately was able to help. Whether it was giving a young couple medicine on credit for their first child or trying to get someone through the "12 step" program after receiving a call in the small hours of the morning, he was about helping others. Regardless of what issues in life he faced, his love of people was beyond reproach.

It is funny how God can take any person and use them to help others along this way. Sometimes, the real benefit of a life does not come into clear view until after the person is gone; that is the case with him. In spite of his shortcomings or personal faults, one thing can be said without reservation: he loved people.

May each of us examine ourself. May we see that person in need of help or encouragement and not only notice, but also offer a helping hand. That is what he did. May we not allow our own shortcomings to keep us from ultimately making, and leaving, this world better than when we came into it. If this record of our father's last days helps us to do that, then its purpose will have been accomplished. May God help us to make it so in all of our lives.

For As Long As I Can

All the world's a stage,
And all the men and women merely players.
They have their exits and their entrances;
And one man in his time plays many parts...
—William Sheakespeare
As You Like It, Act 2, Scene 7

ACT 1
NOVEMBER

SETTING THE STAGE

Life is pleasant. Death is peaceful.
It's the transition that's troublesome.

—Isaac Asimov

CHAPTER 1

SUNDAY, NOVEMBER 28

It Begins

Daddy was moved from *Westchester Manor* nursing home to *High Point Regional Hospital* on Sunday, November 28th. He came to the nursing home on the 16th of November around 1:00 p. m., arriving by ambulance from Lumberton. He fell at home on November 2nd and stayed in the hospital in Lumberton until his arrival in High Point.

He has been in room 108 at the nursing home. At this time, we are holding his bed in hopes that he can return there. He has been doing well with physical therapy, but has virtually no movement in his lower extremities.

His inability to move either feet or legs is very unsettling to me. Is more going on here than it appears?

* * *

David and Lynda arrived for a visit with Daddy at the nursing home just after lunch. They found him sitting in his "gerry chair," having had a good lunch and looking quite refreshed. They brought the shoes he requested and a small Christmas tree for his room. It was a nice visit.

After the staff put him back to bed, I noticed that an earlier cough had gotten worse. He has had a cough ever since he arrived.

It was minimal, but over the weekend has grown more noticeable. We had both the hall and floor nurses to take a look at him. The floor nurse agreed his cough was bad and that he sounded congested. His temperature was 100.1; she called the hospital. The doctor felt that Daddy should go to the ER, so they picked him up by ambulance around 3:30. I rode with David and Lynda to the hospital. When we arrived, I checked us into the ER. Soon thereafter, David and I took turns going in to see Daddy. He was in room 19 and on oxygen; his level was 93. I was there when Dr. Chen came in to see Daddy. He rolled him on his side to examine his bedsore, repeating the process on the other side. He questioned us about Daddy's situation and asked him to move his legs. Daddy could not.

Dr. Chen told us that Daddy had a UTI (urinary tract infection), plus pneumonia, and that he would admit him. He is more concerned about why Daddy has no use of his legs than the other issues at this point. Riding with David and Lynda, we left the hospital to return to the nursing home to get my car. David and Lynda would leave well after dark to go back to Lumberton. Daddy would be admitted to room 759. I would not sleep well tonight.

CHAPTER 2

MONDAY, NOVEMBER 29

Suspicions

I went to the hospital at lunch and again at supper. The doctor had been by this afternoon. They paged him when I asked, and I was able to speak with him, a Dr. Powell. He informed us that they have found suspicious looking lesions on several of the small bones on Daddy's spine. He didn't suggest anything, but laid out a clear plan of action: MRI (already done), CT scan on Tuesday, full skeletal scan on Wednesday and a possible biopsy on Thursday or Friday. Daddy is not overly alarmed, but obviously the news is not what we hoped to hear at this point.

CHAPTER 3

TUESDAY, NOVEMBER 30

Uncertainty

I saw him again at lunch and supper. His appetite is good. I found him a bit hoarse from his breathing treatment (2 times a day), but upbeat. He had the CT scan before lunch and the doctor came by just for a moment to talk with him around 3:00, but with no real news. I asked them to contact the doctor for me. She called the hall phone around 7:00 to report what the CT scan revealed. Daddy has lesions on his spine that appear to be tumors. He also has a small nodule in his upper right lung. I asked her to tell him on Wednesday; she could explain it better than I. She is suspicious of some form of cancer, but unsure at this time. Suddenly, my throat had a lump in it. I hung up the phone (just outside of Daddy's room) and went in to speak to him. He said, "Tell me the news, good, bad or indifferent." I told him about the spinal findings, but not about the lung. He said, "I thought as much." He became a bit emotional, but continued to be controlled and optimistic.

We talked until close to 8:00, mainly about spiritual issues. He assured me that he is ready to die. He desires that God's will be done, whatever that is. Somewhere in our discussion, he wanted to know about what John Wesley said just before he died. I told him, "But the best of all is, God is with us." He likes that and said he wanted to remember it. He told me to remember it as well. It was clear that he was referring to its use in his potential funeral. I told him I would remember. We talked about how God led him to High Point for this time, knowing that he would find the spiritual encouragement and help that he needed. I told him about the assurance of God, another Wesleyan distinctive. He quoted the words, "Blessed assurance, Jesus is mine." He couldn't remember the rest of the words, so I finished it for him:

> *Blessed Assurance, Jesus is mine,*
> *O What a foretaste of glory divine.*
> *Heir of salvation, purchased of God,*
> *Born of His Spirit, washed in His blood.*

He liked that. As we talked about other issues, he made the statement that we work all of our lives to secure material things, only to leave them. "That little piece of real estate that I have worked so much at in Lumberton came from God, and goes back to Him." I had read from 2 Corinthians, chapters 4 and 5 the previous night and we had talked about how the body wastes away, but we will receive a greater glory. Tonight, we both were tearful, but not overly sad. He talked about his children, saying, "If it takes my death to bring my children together, then that makes me happy." He said again, "I am not afraid to die." He clearly has a peace that comes from God.

In the midst of our conversations, dietary called to find out what he wanted for supper. He ordered meatloaf, green beans, grapes, a banana, roll, tea and coffee. He ate the banana first and jokingly said, "Yes, we have no bananas." I helped him get his tray situated and he ate like it was good.

I told him I viewed our time together as a gift from God and that I could clearly see Him working out getting him to this place. I shared with him how for months my prayer had been that his heart would be soft. I told him that is exactly how I found him that first day he came to the nursing home two weeks ago. We both rejoiced.

Before I left, he asked me to bring his glasses from the nursing home when I came back the next day.

I feel compelled to begin a folder, even now, in preparation for his funeral. I want to gather some thoughts together, as well as anything else that I think he would want me to know. While I left him with a heavy heart, as I think about his spiritual future, I rejoice in spirit. I slept well.

ACT 2
DECEMBER

ADJUSTING THE SCRIPT

Because I could not stop for Death —
He kindly stopped for me —
The carriage held but just ourselves
And immortality.

—Emily Dickinson

CHAPTER 4

WEDNESDAY, DECEMBER 1

God is With Us

When I arrived at the hospital today, Daddy was working on lunch. It was not as good as last night, tasting like "hospital" food. Nevertheless, he ate his meatloaf again and did very well.

He had one breathing treatment today and is still a bit hoarse. His cough actually sounds better it seems. They had given him some type of injection to assist with the imaging of the full body scan. He joked with his nurse, and me, about being "electric." I brought his mail; he had two cards from people in Lumberton. He was very appreciative of their thoughtfulness. I read the cards to him and put them back in the bag with his glasses, placing them in the drawer by his bed for "future reference." As he finished his meal, we talked about things.

He feels encouragement from the person who discussed the upcoming full body skeletal scan with him. The doctor said he really wasn't sure what the CT scan showed; it was inconclusive. While it could be some type of damage, it may not necessarily be cancer. Again, Daddy expressed that he accepts the outcome, whatever it may indicate. We know that they will probably do a biopsy by the weekend, thereby giving us a clear diagnosis.

After telling him that I wanted to discuss something with him, he said that he wanted to talk to me, too. It became clear that we both were on the same page as we talked. I wanted him to know that while we do not know what the ultimate outcome will be, I want what is best for him. *If* it seems that therapy will not benefit him, the family will probably want him to be closer to them. He expressed that he really didn't want to be stuck in a room in someone's house, but would take whatever action was needed. At this point, it is too early to tell what the ultimate outcome will be. I wanted him to know that regardless of what is decided, I do not feel it is my decision, or any other family member's decision, but his. I expressed that I wanted to be fair to the rest of the family. He said that he wants to make sure they understand that regardless of where he ultimately ends up, I did not unduly influence him to stay in High Point, either in the hospital or the nursing home. That said, we agreed that we understood each other.

He asked me once more about the John Wesley statement. I quoted it again, "But the best of all is, God is with us." He again stated that he wanted me to remember those words. I told him that I researched it this morning and had found the full account of John Wesley's last days. I said I would bring him the quote. He said to bring the whole article (off the Internet). "I love historical things," he said. I assured him that I would do so.

At 12:45, they came to take him for his full skeletal scan. Handing me his teeth, I put them in the cup and told him I would let them soak and have them ready for supper. He told the two attendants who came to get him that I was his son and his counselor. I offered a brief prayer while I took his left hand in both of my hands before leaving. I said that I loved him and would see him for supper. The doctor had not spoken to him personally about the CT scan yet. I pray that he gets a good report.

* * *

I went back to the hospital at approximately 5:30. I found Daddy in good spirits. He had several items of good news. His oxygen level has been as high as 98. His bedsores are continuing to improve. The pulmonary doctor wants to take a biopsy as soon as possible, but is not overly concerned according to Daddy. He did not hear from the bone scan today and we were told that they would give a report on Thursday. We do not know what the results of either test will ultimately be, but are hopeful.

Myra Snider, a good friend and my former secretary, had been by today and had a good visit, bringing Daddy a balloon. While I was there, Bill Eudy, whose wife is a resident at the nursing home, visited. He is always funny and prayed a beautiful prayer with Daddy. Daddy continues to express trust in God.

For supper, he had spaghetti and salad with toast. He ate well. He also has a pulse in both feet, something he has not had recently. He told me that his feet are warm; I felt them and they were indeed very warm. He is able to pull himself up using his arms as well, moving from side to side. A very pleasant nurse came to give him 3 units of insulin. His sugar is up, possibly from his medications as well as the pneumonia, which is better. She was very knowledge-able about moving him to make him comfortable. After he pulled himself in place by using his arms, he ate a good supper.

His pneumonia is improving and his white blood count is down. David called and we shared the improvements with him. He was pleased that he had filled over 260 prescriptions today. But he did express to me his concerns about the potential findings of the biopsy. I told him that I shared his concern, but was hopeful that the results from the scan and the biopsy will be negative. Around 7:30, they came to give Daddy a breathing treatment, which makes him hoarse. Before I left him, he told me that he loved me and I said I loved him. I will see him for lunch tomorrow. By then, I trust that he will have a report on his scan, "good, bad or indifferent." I feel like God has given us a gift, regardless of the outcome of the rest of this week.

CHAPTER 5

FRIDAY, DECEMBER 3

The Procedures Begin

I went home to Rose Hill yesterday after visiting Daddy for lunch. He has not heard any news as of today. I called him around 5:45 while I was on the road. (Cindy was visiting her parents over the Thanksgiving weekend; I had gone to get her.) He did not have his biopsy yesterday, but will probably have it today.

* * *

Cindy and I headed back to High Point at 11:00 a. m. I received a voice mail on my cell phone as we neared Asheboro. The nurse had called to inform me that nothing was wrong. Not understanding her point, I called back and after several rings, Daddy answered and told me that they were going to take him for a biopsy on his right lung as well as possibly check some of the fluid in both lungs. He was a bit apprehensive I was later to discover.

After going to the house, unloading our stuff, and getting our dog Odie situated, we got to the hospital at approximately 5:15. Daddy was having his procedure done and not available in his room. I was able to have a nurse page his doctor. The doctor soon called the nurses' station and I spoke with her. The bone scan from earlier in the week did not reveal anything of immediate concern, but the biopsy will reveal any cancer, if it is present. It will probably be up to the pulmonary doctor to decide when Daddy can leave the hospital. The biopsy will reveal its results in three to four days. They will not keep him during that time unless medically necessary.

Daddy came back to the room at 6:00, wheezy, but otherwise doing well. They got him situated and told him that he could have clear liquids. Around 6:30, he ate an orange popsicle, broth and Jell-O. His appetite is good. He later ate spaghetti and salad yet again. His sugar, after his meal, was 175; his oxygen is up to 100% with no fever.

Harold, the pharmacist Daddy helped through addiction, called tonight, along with David, Carol and Ashly, Mike and Carol's only daughter. (She and her husband live in Arizona.) Daddy spoke to Carol and Ashly, but had Harold and David to call him back tomorrow. I also talked with Carol, who is coming Sunday, and later Ashly. Daddy was glad to hear from all of them.

Cindy went to the hospital snack shop to get us something to eat. We ate cheese toast, potato chips, and diet Pepsi in the room as Daddy finished his meal. He was talkative, but soon grew sleepy.

We thought that the pulmonary doctor was coming by, but we left the hospital about 8:30 without seeing him. Daddy said it would be Monday before we got a report and at least Monday before he goes back to the nursing home. We adjusted his "blue blanket" and turned off the lights before leaving. The blanket was a gift from David and Lynda; it came with him from Lumberton. He looked very restful after a busy day and a very full supper.

CHAPTER 6

SATURDAY, DECEMBER 4

One of the Hardest Things

By 12:15, Cindy and I were at the hospital. Daddy was dozing, waiting for his lunch. He had been in pain earlier, and had been given pain medication. He was now comfortable and seemed well. It is obvious that his pneumonia is better. His cough doesn't rattle like it had and he hasn't been running a fever for three days or so.

His lunch came about 12:30. He had beef tips over noodles, carrots, milk and coffee. We had to remind them to bring it; they had forgotten. He had me to get his tray ready, using any spices they included as well as Sweet-n-Low and creamer in his coffee. As he ate, he received a call from David. He and Lynda are going to Mama's and Ronald's this afternoon in Wallace for a visit. They plan to order plates from the "Pink Supper House" and go to Sammy's to eat supper this evening. (The Pink Supper House is a community barbeque restaurant that is only open on Saturday evenings. It is run by one of the local church's ladies group and raises money for the church, as well as other community needs. It has been a community institution for decades. Daddy's mother, Vada, worked there many years ago.)

Daddy gave David a good word, telling him that he was comfortable and enjoying his lunch. After the conversation ended, Daddy ate while I talked with David. David is still concerned about the biopsy. He also wants me to let him know if I hear of any "bad" news relative to Daddy. I assured him I would. He said that Daddy would not tell me if he received bad news. Up to this point, the news about his immediate needs has been very positive.

David told me he would leave the *Sam's Drug Store "Carolina"* basketball calendars with Sammy, who would bring them to me when he comes to High Point to visit Daddy. The calendars are poster size on heavy stock paper and include photos of the team and coaches. *Sam's Drug Store*, with the appropriate phone numbers, is printed at the bottom. The posters are highly collectible to UNC basketball fans. The store generally has about 100 on hand each year to give to customers. (My secretary, Carla, requested a couple for her husband, Brad. He already was given one by me and was thrilled. He has a couple of friends who would like one as well.) That being said, David reminded me that *Carolina* was playing on TV today. I retrieved the *UNC* pocket calendar from my billfold and found that they were playing Kentucky on CBS; a 12:00 start. *Kentucky* is ranked # 8, *Carolina* # 11. Cindy and I watched the game with Daddy, talking through much of it.

He talked about some of the early teams and players. Daddy doesn't care for sports, except *Carolina* basketball. *UNC* won by 7 or 8 points, a minor upset. For the last few minutes of the game, the respiratory therapist gave him a breathing treatment; Daddy doesn't mind. He is agreeable to most every thing they do. As the game was ending, the therapist removed the mask used for the treatment and hooked up Daddy's oxygen again. It was obvious that Daddy was once again full and sleepy. I told him I would either be back, or would call him later this evening. He said he was comfortable, but asked that we pull his "blue blanket" up over his shoulders and turn out the lights. He wanted the TV to remain on. He said he would like to listen to the Army/Navy football game. Daddy looked very comfortable as we left him. I told him I loved him and he said that he loved me, and Cindy, as well.

Upon leaving, Cindy and I went to the 6th floor to visit Grace Allison, a patient in the hospital who is from our church. After a good visit with her, I spotted Dr. Powell and asked if I could speak with him. While I was under the assumption that the bone scan didn't reveal any cancer, he said that he had actually talked with

Daddy about "end of life" issues. The bone scan revealed some issues with a rib and two places on his back. He very clearly stated that they expect to find cancer in the biopsy. If they do, then no further tests will probably be done. I asked him about the plans if no cancer is found. He said that a bone biopsy of the rib would probably be in order, but he doesn't expect the need to do one, saying that it was only a last resort, since it is quite painful. He stated that Daddy wanted him to be very truthful with him and I assured him that is the way Daddy sees it and wants it. He said that we should hear from the biopsy by Tuesday at the latest. When I asked how long before Daddy leaves the hospital, he said the middle or end of next week. *If* the biopsy(s) reveal no cancer, then neurological testing would possibly be an option. He sees no reason why Daddy cannot feel or move his feet and legs. I remarked to him that his comments were very sobering, but I appreciated his honesty. While Daddy will not admit, or even mention, that he has cancer until the end (to protect me? the rest of the family?), it appears that David's caution is correct. Daddy wants to make his own decisions and doesn't want to burden me, or the rest of his children, as long as he can make his own decisions. He told me that just this week. While I want him to make his own decisions, I want to *fully* know the truth of the situation. Cindy and I left the hospital with little more conversation. My optimism over Daddy's physical prognosis earlier in the day has turned to melancholy.

After arriving at home, I felt that I should call David. I called Mama and talked with her, as David and Lynda hadn't arrived yet. Ronald is doing well and had his second chemotherapy treatment in Kinston yesterday. She and I talked about the happenings of the day. She was very comforting and also expressed her concern for me, and all of us, as only a mother can. While we talked, David and Lynda arrived. I could hear them in the background as she greeted them. David took the phone.

I think telling him the news about Daddy's situation, especially after we were encouraged earlier, was one of the hardest things I have *ever* had to do. I remember how sad David said he was the day Daddy left Lumberton, knowing that he and Daddy have worked together so closely for these last 14 years or so. I can only imagine his concern for Daddy, as well as his questions about the future of the drug store. What we thought was Daddy's chance for independence may instead be the last stage of his earthly life. I still know in my heart that God brought him to High Point for a greater purpose than simply *physical* healing.

David said that he would tell Sammy tonight about the current state of affairs, but he doesn't want to tell Lynda yet. He realizes how much it will upset her. We talked about how to tell Carol when she gets here to visit tomorrow. David suggested that I tell her on her way out of the hospital, or at least when she is out of Daddy's room. We know she will naturally be very upset. I hate to tell her, but know that she needs to be told. I pray she will be all right.

I called Daddy at the hospital after my conversation with David. He said that he had ordered his supper, but not eaten it yet. He had ordered spaghetti yet again; he *really* likes spaghetti. The pulmonary doctor had been by and given him a good report. I told Daddy that I had spoken to Dr. Powell since I had seen him earlier today and gave him the report on what he had told me. Daddy acknowledged that while my account of their conversation was true, he didn't want to alarm anyone and still holds out hope that all of the tests will be negative. I got a little tearful and told him that I loved him and would do *anything* in the world for him. He shared my concern about Carol and how to address it with her tomorrow. He suggested that we be honest and frank with her, but stressed that we still don't know anything for certain. He did concede that the doctors were leaning towards cancer and not simply suspicious of it. He said that he had fought a good fight and that he would fight more, for as long as he could. I am sure that he could detect the sorrow and sadness in my voice. He told me that I don't need to worry about him, relative to his death. He is ready to meet the Lord. (In the midst of our sorrow, God's ultimate purposes are accomplished!) I praise God for what has happened to Daddy since he has arrived in High Point. While he came here for physical help, little did any of us realize that he would be receiving that which will get him through death's door and beyond.

While my heart is heavy at the *potential* news Monday or Tuesday, I do praise God for Daddy's spiritual testimony. If it took all of this to get him to heaven, then it is ultimately worth it. Eternity is forever; these bodies are not made to last forever. Daddy further commented that he realizes the doctors can't keep him going indefinitely. That is true, but I know that his spirit and soul will forever be in God's presence; his testimony confirms it. Our sadness is earthbound only.

CHAPTER 7

SUNDAY, DECEMBER 5

A Gift from God

W hen Cindy and I arrived at the hospital, Mike and Carol had just gotten there. We went in and greeted everyone. Daddy was finishing his lunch and seemed as talkative as ever. Carol and I looked out of the window at the view. Daddy is on the 7th floor (759) and the view is really nice. You can see downtown well. I pointed out the First Methodist church, the First Baptist church and the GE financial building.

Carol made a comment as we stood near the window out of earshot. She said the nurse had mentioned that Daddy could have OxyContin for pain if needed. Carol told her that he shouldn't need it. The nurse said that they normally gave it to the cancer patients. Carol mentioned again that he didn't need it. She was curious as to why they would offer it to him. I told her that I needed to talk with her. She, Cindy, and I went down the hall to the waiting room. I told Carol about my discussion with Dr. Powell last evening. She was controlled, but we both shed a few tears. We talked about telling Scott this week. She is going to fly out in the morning from Raleigh to spend most of the week in Tennessee visiting him. She plans to return to High Point on Saturday to visit Daddy. By then, surely he will be out of the hospital and we will know more about his status and prognosis. After 30 minutes or so, Carol composed herself and we went back to his room. She handled it even better than I had expected, but did state that Mike would have to "push me on the plane in the morning." She also said that I had better be praying hard for her then. I hate to see her cry, but we both agreed that it was the right thing to tell her about Daddy's potential diagnosis and getting everything in the open. While we both know that the outcome is not yet sure, she agreed with me that the prognosis and probable diagnosis do not look good. I told her that I see my time with Daddy, at the least, as a gift from God and that we have made significant strides to get him strong spiritually. I shared that he had assured me over and over that he was not afraid to die and that he was indeed ready to go to heaven. She was very encouraged by that.

When we got back to the room, Mike and Daddy were watching a Mike Myers movie that was actually quite serious. We talked for a good while about various things, mostly light-hearted stuff. Carol did not tell Daddy that she knew about his situation. Eventually, she and Mike began to prepare to leave. I asked them if they wanted to go by *Krispy Kreme* and get a doughnut and coffee. They agreed that they would like that. I told Daddy that I would bring him some coffee, asking him if he wanted mild or bold. He said, "Bold." Cindy and I excused ourselves and went back to the waiting room to wait for them, the same room in which we had held our sobering conversation earlier. I thought that Carol might want to talk with Daddy alone.

After 10 minutes or so, the four of us left the hospital and went to the *Krispy Kreme* doughnut shop. Cindy ordered a doughnut and small frozen latte. Carol and Mike ordered four doughnuts total. He had coffee and she had a diet Coke. I had an apple-filled doughnut and a medium bold coffee. Their coffee is so good.

As we finished, Carol and I stood by the window overlooking the production of the doughnuts and talked. She told me that she felt good about Daddy being with me here in High Point. She was glad that he was not going to die all alone in his apartment in Lumberton, unprepared to meet God. She also feels that he should stay in High Point so he will have good care, both physically and spiritually. She shed tears as we talked, but expressed her love for Daddy, telling me again that she was glad Cindy and I are with him. We walked out together after I got a refill of coffee and bought one just like it for Daddy.

* * *

On arriving back at Daddy's room, we found him comfortable. The nurse informed me that she had changed his bandages on his bedsores and gotten him settled. The light was off and the TV was on. He smiled and welcomed us back. He wanted the coffee, so I poured some in a cup. He drank about one-half of the total amount, smiling as he said, "Now that is *real* coffee." He seemed to enjoy it very much. He had already placed the order for his supper.

The pulmonary doctor came in and had Daddy to turn on his side so he could listen to his lungs. Daddy turned on his left side, with some effort, and allowed the doctor to listen to his lungs from the back. When he was done, the doctor said that Daddy was fine as far as his pneumonia is concerned and that his work is basically done. It was good to hear this news and Daddy remarked as the doctor left, "One down, two to go." We both smiled.

Daddy's supper soon arrived. He had ordered meatloaf, potatoes and slaw; he also had milk and coffee. They failed to send the ketchup he requested, so Cindy phoned them, but Daddy finished his meal before the ketchup arrived. He said that the slaw "helped the meatloaf." He also ate a bowl of tomato soup. Once again, his appetite is very good.

I told him that Carol knew everything we knew. He was optimistic, but again acknowledged that he realized cancer was a possibility. I read from the *Light from the Word* devotional and the scripture that it recommended. The devotional is produced by our denomination. I used the Gideon bible in his room for the scripture reading. The devotion was on God's grace. I had brought the devotional today, along with the bulletins from both the Celebration and Heritage worship services at our church. The Celebration service is our large service, while the Heritage service is fairly small, comprised of senior adults. He said that he would probably want to begin reading again after Tuesday. I told him I could get him more reading material, both religious and non-religious. He reminded me that he didn't mind getting religious literature, needing all of it that "I can get."

After the devotional, we realigned his head some, got his TV situated and turned down the lights. He told me that he loved me as

I kissed his forehead and said goodnight. I informed him that I would ask them about shaving him in the morning and washing his hair, which I did as we left his hall. Cindy also hugged him as he said that he loved us both. I could feel the emotion in his voice. He is a very appreciative person and rarely complains. I again thank God for this time together. I hope to visit him for supper tomorrow night, but will not be able to visit him at lunch as we have an all-day staff meeting.

CHAPTER 8

TUESDAY, DECEMBER 7

Rollercoaster Ride

Today was a rollercoaster ride. While I was at the hospital during lunch (I slipped away from our staff meeting), the pulmonary doctor came to see Daddy. He said that he had looked at the tests from yesterday. One oncologist said that the test was negative, while the other said it was inconclusive. The doctor put a positive spin on it and said that they wanted to do a biopsy from the outside, using the CT scan as a guide. He was optimistic that they would not find anything unusual. I felt encouraged! The biopsy yet to be done was to ensure that a larger, and therefore better, sample base was available from which to work. Again, I was led to believe that it was precautionary and not to expect any differing results. As he ate his lunch, I left and called David. I also called Sammy's house and talked with Sandra as well. Carol called later in the evening.

I told them that things were looking good, relative to his lung. I also told them that I did not expect any bad or questionable news about his lungs. I was to be sobered.

* * *

This evening, I went back to the hospital for his supper, feeling encouraged. Based on the optimism of the pulmonary doctor earlier today, Daddy had even said that he felt confident he would eventually walk again. He realizes it may be with a walker, but that would thrill him, if that is how it is to be. I asked for the nurse to page his primary doctor, so they paged Dr. Chen. I took his phone call in the hallway just outside of Daddy's room. My optimism, while not uncalled for, was soon dealt a "reality check" blow. Dr. Chen said that there are basically three types of biopsy:

> <u>Tracheal</u>— *Daddy had this procedure; it is taken through the nose.*
> <u>Entrance from the outside</u>— *He will have that this week.*
> <u>Surgery</u>— *They go in and remove a section of the organ in question, in this case, the right lung.*

Each one has a better chance of securing larger samples of material, respectively, and therefore produces better results. The material from the tracheal procedure did not gather a large enough sample to gain a conclusive result. Daddy's situation, in other words, is no worse, but no better either. The doctor also used the word "cancer" several times. The bottom line: the primary care physician team is almost certain that Daddy has cancer, but cannot make a positive diagnosis *yet*. When I asked him what would happen if the second procedure comes back with inconclusive results, he said that the third procedure is not an option. Daddy would probably never come off of the respirator after the surgery. Checking the bones could be an option, but he is concerned that the bone may be too soft from cancer and that even if they could find solid bone, the sample would not accurately reflect possible cancer. Plus, he said that trying to put a biopsy needle in the bone could be like "pushing a needle through drywall." I asked him if he was still leaning towards a cancer diagnosis and he said, "Yes." According to him, if the cancer cannot be detected with these limited biopsies, then we may have to go with no clear diagnosis. He feels confident that the biopsy to come (from the outside) will be conclusive, one way or another.

I went back to the room and filled Daddy in on the report. He already knows their leanings, but will not openly talk about it, as long as they have no clear diagnosis. He is the most persistently optimistic person that I know. He received calls from Mr. Lowry and then David almost immediately after he hung up. (Mr. Lowry has been doing relief work at the drug store for years and is a dear friend to Daddy. He has been helping David at the store during Daddy's absence.)

I spoke with David and I know he could tell something in my voice had changed. Even though they all know about Daddy's new biopsy, I surely, albeit innocently, gave them false hope. I didn't want to contradict Daddy's positive slant, so I gave the phone to him and told David that I would speak to him later. David obviously questioned Daddy about any news he had received. Daddy insisted that he felt better and that they were leaning toward not finding anything. While he doesn't share non-truths about his situation, he also doesn't paint as dark a scenario as the primary care doctors are suggesting at this point.

After he hung up the phone, I told him I was concerned that we be realistic with the others in our reporting of news. He emphasized that they do not know his full status at this point. While *technically* this is correct, it is not a "complete" picture. He and I talked about not simply giving opinions, but reporting facts when we have them. I agree. I felt better after clarifying things with him. Cindy and I soon left, but before we did, I read him his mail. He received four cards, all from people in Lumberton. He enjoyed hearing from the various persons, making comments about each as they were mentioned. Cindy and I both kissed him goodnight and left. I did pray with him; he liked that.

* * *

When I got home, I called David to clarify that while the biopsy was negative and/or inconclusive, it was because of the small sample size and not because it was definitely negative or inconclusive. He totally understood. I agreed to only report clear and definitive news from now on. We talked about being on a "rollercoaster ride" and trying to avoid it by not being up or down until we have a clear understanding of what is going on with Daddy.

I also told him that Dr. Chen plans to have a urologist change out Daddy's catheter. Daddy will need to have a "pick" line for 14 days after his second biopsy is done. They want to give him intravenous antibiotics through it. I told Daddy that I didn't know if our nursing home could maintain such a line. I told David Dr. Chen had said that Daddy could stay in the hospital for that period of time. Daddy has said that he indeed wants to stay in the hospital for those 14 days, if necessary. He does not want to lose his room at *Westchester Manor* nursing home, affirming that was the reason he came. David agreed with the potentially longer hospital stay and said that he appreciated what I was doing for Daddy. I assured him that I considered it a privilege. I will fill in Sammy; he is to be here Thursday and Friday. I will also explain the present situation to Carol, who is coming Saturday. For now, however, no news means just that, "no news."

At this juncture, I can tell that all of this is slowly taking an emotional toll on me. I am not sleeping well and am tired a lot. I also am a bit short with Cindy. While my shortness is not terribly pronounced, I am not myself completely. She is trying to get Christmas decorations up, though I am not very interested. I suppose the diversion would do me good, but I feel like I need to maintain close contact with Daddy, thus every night from 5:15 to 7:00 or 7:30, we are at the hospital. While I love being with him and am doing all I can to keep him encouraged, I can tell that I need to go on with my life as much as is reasonably possible. I love Daddy and hate to see him suffering, but I need to keep a healthy perspective...and outlook on things. I know that Cindy is impacted as well.

I want to continue to think about the positive things that are happening:

> *Daddy's pain is under control.*
> *His pneumonia is better.*
> *The hospital care could not be better.*
> *He is encouraging himself and does not feel sorry for himself (that could be a problem).*
> *He is not terribly depressed.*

The doctors are doing all they can to diagnose and help him.

Spiritually, he continues to be positive and rely on God. He is at peace with life...or death.

We still talk about that while he came to High Point for physical therapy, it is obvious that there is a bigger picture being addressed here...and God is working. He continues to see that and expresses his faith in Christ and wants God's will to be done.

"Lord, give me the stamina that I see displayed in my father. Amen."

CHAPTER 9

WEDNESDAY, DECEMBER 8

Running on Both Arms

Cindy and I went to check on Daddy after the Senior Adult luncheon at *Canterbury's* restaurant today. The restaurant is part of the *Providence Place* campus complex of our church. The dinners are a nice diversion and are held once a month there. I was going to visit Daddy a little later, but decided to go and see how he was earlier than planned. I knew he was going to have the second biopsy because I talked with Dr. Skaggs, the radiologist. He needed my permission to perform the procedure. The doctor mentioned Daddy's "history of Alzheimer's" and that he is on pain medication that requires permission from someone responsible for him. Of course, Daddy was fully aware of the procedure today, so I gave my consent over the phone. The other day, he said that the mention of Alzheimer's would follow him the rest of his life; apparently he is right. It is obvious, I might add, that Alzheimer's does not appear to affect him at this time and his thinking seems very clear.

Daddy was just returning to his room. We saw them remove the gurney, but couldn't see Daddy because the door was closed. Cindy and I sat in the room near it and waited. Soon Dr. Chen came by to see Daddy and spoke to us in the empty, adjacent room. He said they felt good about the procedure, and he felt good personally that they would have results by Friday, or Monday at the latest. I asked him several questions and he told me the following:

They feel certain that Daddy has cancer.

Cancer appears to be in his lung and on several bones. He has places on his spine, described as "peppered" by the doctor.

The cancer is the apparent cause of his inability to walk. Dr. Chen said that some of the cancer may be undetectable since it is so small, but it could be pressing on Daddy's spinal cord.

If the lung biopsy comes back negative, the chances of getting a bone sample from his spine are remote. The cancer may have weakened the bone and there is no room for error when trying to gain access to bone material near the spinal cord. He is not sure of where to go if we get a negative reading.

If Daddy has lung cancer, his time to live is limited to weeks or months. His probable type of lung cancer (small-cell) tends to be both aggressive and fast.

He finally stated that Daddy should return to the nursing home on Monday after he finishes days 10-14 of his antibiotic IV. If cancer is found, he will be scheduled to see an oncologist in the days ahead. His potential cancer may be slowed, but not stopped.

Cindy and I went in with Dr. Chen to see Daddy. He had actually returned from his follow-up x-ray to make sure his lung was okay from the procedure earlier this morning. Obviously, everything is fine. Dr. Chen looked at Daddy briefly and asked him to move his toes, to try hard. He could not.

After the doctor left, I read Daddy his mail. He had four cards, all from Lumberton. He likes getting cards and telling me about who the various people are. We did not stay long. I cleaned his teeth and got them put in for supper to come. As usual, he was restful, but a bit tired from his busy day. I combed his hair and left him in a comfortable position.

* * *

I went back this evening as he was finishing the last of his supper. According to the ticket, it was meatloaf again! I commented on it and he said that the food was good and "Meatloaf is hard to beat." He ate everything and was enjoying his coffee when I arrived.

The routine was much the same as many other visits: I combed his hair and brushed his teeth and put them in the container to soak. In the middle of my arriving and leaving, however, we had an entertaining conversation. He thought that they were removing the catheter without replacing it. I explained that a urologist was to remove "and replace" it. Daddy got tickled and joked about running on "both arms" if anyone else other than a urologist tried to insert another catheter. He laughed and asked me if I had ever seen anyone "run on his arms?" He said that it felt good to laugh.

Pearl Harbor Day was yesterday, so we talked about what he was doing on Dec. 7, 1941. He was 14 years old and playing on the "home place" at Northeast with others his age. Our conversation gradually turned towards the present. He wanted to talk about how he was feeling right now. He described the peace that he has. He reiterated that he couldn't understand it, but that he feels at peace. He knows his life is in God's hands, whether he lives or dies. He asked me, or rather stated, that "Not everyone in my situation has this peace, do they?" I assured him that they did not, but that we know it comes from God. He became tearful. I handed him a napkin from the holder by the sink.

I told him how much God loves him and all of us. I said, "Daddy, God loves you very much." He smiled several times and said that he knew his peace was a result of God's grace. He quoted the words, "Amazing Grace, how sweet the sound...." I assured him that he, nor any of us, can ever understand God's grace; we just accept it. He agreed.

We also talked about how God uses suffering to reveal Himself. I told him about C. S. Lewis and his book *Surprised by Joy*. He said he hoped to read it "If I ever get the opportunity." Our conversation was very encouraging. Daddy is at peace; of that I am certain. I shared again how God uses suffering to draw us to Himself. It was obvious that Daddy understands that more than a lot of people.

I am continually encouraged! Daddy is ready to go to heaven if God calls. I am certain of that. I thank God and praise Him for His workings in Daddy's life to bring him to this place of peace.

CHAPTER 10

THURSDAY, DECEMBER 9

The Results Are In

I am sitting in the *Starbucks* coffee shop located at *Barnes and Noble* here in High Point. It has been a rather eventful day. I just left Daddy at the hospital and will go back in a while; it is presently 3:30. I know that Sammy, Sandra and Vada are on the way, as they plan to visit with Daddy today and tomorrow. Sammy said that they might want to go to the hospital first and then call me after they get there.

David just called my cell phone to follow-up on a call that I made to him earlier. I filled him in and began writing. The day's events are as follows:

I went to the hospital, arriving at 12:15. Daddy had an egg salad sandwich and some green beans for lunch. He didn't seem to be that hungry, but ate about one-half of it. He asked me what they put into egg salad to make it taste so bland? He then smiled. I lowered his head and dimmed the lights before I left. Before that time, he had his catheter changed out. They pre-medicated him through the "pick" in his left front shoulder, and he was almost instantly calmer than usual. I talked with the urologist as he got his materials together. He is from St. Petersburg, Florida and knows Pastor Paul, who is on staff at our church. As he got ready to do the procedure, I left the room.

After ten minutes, the urologist came out and said that it went well. Daddy told me that he had been apprehensive about this day for five weeks, but that it was no problem at all. (The initial catheter insertion in Lumberton had been *exceptionally* painful.) He commented on how gentle the doctor was. We both felt relieved that it was over.

As stated above, with lunch over and a new catheter in, I left him resting peacefully. I went to the Centennial campus office for the afternoon. Our church has senior adult housing on two campuses. I keep Thursday afternoon office hours on the Centennial campus. I was paged within 10 minutes after arriving at my office so I called back and it was Dr. Chen. He told me that the pathology report was back and Daddy does have lung cancer. He said that the oncologist and he were going to tell Daddy the findings. I had told him earlier to let me know when the results were in so that I could be there with Daddy. I informed him that I could be there in 15 minutes; he said they would wait.

I called Cindy on the way to the hospital and told her the news. She was obviously sorry to hear it. I hung up as I arrived at the hospital.

I went up to Daddy's room and found him resting on his right side. I asked him if he had seen the doctor, and he said he had seen the urologist 30 minutes earlier. He said he had not seen Dr. Chen today. Hearing this, I went to the nurse and asked her to page Dr. Chen. In just a moment he came, along with Dr. Williford, the oncologist. She told me what they found and the probable course of action from here. I asked her what the prognosis for life expectancy was, and she said "Several weeks to short months." We went in to talk to Daddy.

He was in the same position he was in when I left him. Dr. Chen asked him how he felt, and as usual Daddy's response was "Pretty good." He is always the optimist! Dr. Chen told him that the pathology report came back positive, and that Dr. Williford was here to tell him about what he should expect. She would also answer any questions he might have.

Her report, in summary, is:

He has stage four lung cancer (has spread to other parts of the body).

The cancer is probably the reason for his fall and also the cause of his inability to walk. She said that the MRI "lit up like a Christmas tree." She was sure it revealed cancer all over his spine.

She told him that he is too sick to endure chemotherapy and would probably not survive the treatments. They would attempt radiation if she thought there was the potential that he would walk again. There really is nowhere to focus the beam because his cancer is so widespread, and there may be several points where small tumors are pressing on his spinal cord.

The level of pain medication that he is on is low, and we could be thankful that he is not in as much pain as he could be.

She feels confident that the doctor at the nursing home could prescribe whatever pain medication he may need.

She mentioned two drugs (of which I cannot remember the names) that might help with his pain. One of them had a 20% chance of shrinking the tumor in his lung, but will not have an effect on his total time left to live. It costs over $2000 per month.

She checked him out and asked him about his present pain. He said that it was "very bearable." She gave me her card and said that she would be off until Monday, but to contact her if we needed anything.

I asked her if she could give Daddy a time-frame from which to work. He did not want to know. He said that he wanted to take it one day at a time, whether one day or one year.

After she left, he and I talked. He told me that he really heard what he basically was expecting to hear. We talked at length about a lot of things, including the gift it has been for him to be here with me. I said that he did not know how thankful I am for this time together. He smiled and said that he did. We talked about how to tell the other children and he told me to go ahead and call David; I said that I would. I also told him that I would call Carol, but would wait to tell Sammy when he arrives this afternoon.

I read from John 14 and 11; he wanted me to read. He spoke again about how much at peace he feels. We both cried a little, but also spoke at length about what heaven might be like, and I encouraged him again to trust God. I asked him *point-blank* if he had invited Jesus into his heart, and he unequivocally answered that he had. He affirmed again that he is ready to die and feels totally at peace as to his preparedness to meet God. Based on his own testimony, *I am certain* that he is ready to go.

I shared how much I will always remember this time that we have had together. He seems to be genuinely pleased that things have worked out for him to be with me for this time. I am in awe of God's provision and presence and at peace relative to Daddy. We both spoke about the sense of calm he feels and how we can have joy, even though we wanted to hear different results. I am confident that the prayers of many for my father have been answered. God is so gracious.

Daddy spoke about not having to feel any regret at this point in his life, almost as a question (I think). I assured him that God does forgive...and forget. He is at peace.

I asked him if he needed anything, or if I could get anything for him. As always, he said, "I have everything I need." He told me that he loved me. I told him I loved him, promising him a cup of *Starbucks* coffee to which he replied, "You better sneak it in." Even in these dire *physical* circumstances, he continues to have a sense of humor.

I went down to the hospital lobby and called David. The conversation was brief. He said he would call me within 30 minutes. He was busy with the store. However, I gave him the main information before I hung up the phone. I then headed to *Barnes and Noble* for a break.

* * *

At the beginning of this writing, David returned my call as I sat at *Barnes and Noble*. He said that he has times where he can talk more freely than others. I tried to give him as much information as I could. He feels that Daddy will want to go back to Lumberton. I told him that I didn't know but was comfortable with whatever Daddy wants to do. I told him that I feel certain that God has accomplished the purpose for which Daddy came to be with Cindy and me. He understood that and said he would talk to Daddy later tonight.

After a bit more writing, I called Carol. She was just getting her things into her room in Knoxville, Tennessee, preparing for the flight back home tomorrow. She had a good visit with Scott. Realizing that she was alone, I hated to give her the news, but was already committed. She took the information well, but became very distraught as our conversation lengthened. I asked her if she still plans to come by High Point on her way to Wallace. She said she would need some time to sort things out and needed to call Mike. I asked her if I did the right thing by calling her, expressing my concern that she was alone. She assured me that I did the right thing. While I hate to see her so upset, I know I did the right thing. She said that she may call me tonight.

I believe I'll get some coffee and head home. I anticipate seeing Sammy and Sandra soon. I want to get Cindy and then head to the hospital to see Daddy after a while.

* * *

Cindy and I returned to the hospital this evening, arriving at approximately 6:00. I anticipated telling Sammy and Sandra the news about Daddy's cancer, but we found them already there. I didn't know if they had been told. Eventually I asked Sammy privately and he told me that Daddy had told them.

We stayed until after 8:00 and spent some good quality time visiting together. We talked about some old times. Throughout the discussions, there were times when everyone was tearful. I can tell that Daddy is more emotional. He does not seem sad per se, but it is clear that he realizes and accepts his cancer and impending death. He continues to have faith and speaks frequently about the feeling of peace that he has. Before we left, we all gathered around him as I led in a prayer, committing all of us to God's grace and strength.

We decided that we would go by *K & W Cafeteria* on the way to our house and eat, but they were locking the door as we went by the entrance. We opted for take-out Chinese near the *K & W*. Bringing it home, we finally started to eat at 9:15. Cindy and Vada baked some chocolate chip cookies we had. We stayed up and talked for a long time. I was as tired as I've ever been in my life when we finally went to bed after midnight.

CHAPTER 11

FRIDAY, DECEMBER 10

Final Plans

This morning, after breakfast at our house, we all rode to the hospital as a group. We stopped by *Providence Place* on the way. I gave Sammy and his family a tour of the facilities. *Providence Place* is the name of our primary church campus. It includes a renovated mall, *Canterbury's* restaurant, the nursing home where Daddy has been living, *First Wesleyan Church* and various types of senior adult housing. My responsibilities to the senior adult community of the church actually take me to both the *Providence Place* and Centennial campuses.

* * *

We arrived at the hospital around lunch. Daddy seemed more down today. He was not sitting up and seemed a bit more subdued, though still optimistic. I asked him at one point if he needed something to help his spirits. He said he was okay and didn't need anything at that time. We talked about a lot of things, including family history relative to our Uncle Butler, as well as other items that were very interesting. We also talked about Daddy's funeral arrangements, which he brought up. He said there were two topics we needed to cover: the funeral and his immediate future. He told us the following:

He will be buried at Cavenaugh's cemetery near Wallace where he already has a plot. The cemetery is the burial place of his parents and three older brothers. Our family has many other members entombed there, some close, some distant kin.

He wasn't sure what to put on his headstone. I reminded him of what he and I talked about earlier, Wesley's statement, "But the best of all is, God is with us." He said that was it. We will plan to put that on his headstone.

Sammy asked him about any music he might want to use. I said "Blessed Assurance" was one we spoke about. Daddy said that would be good and that he didn't have any other songs he especially wanted of which he was aware.

I did ask him about whom he wanted to do the service and he told me that I was the only minister that he really had and he wanted me to do it. I told him that I would be honored and had a lot of encouraging things to say.

Concerning his immediate future, he said that he thought he was where he needed to be. When Sammy asked him about going to Lumberton or even Duplin County, he asked, "What's the point?" He doesn't have any unfinished business. I want him where *he* wants and needs to be. I do not feel strongly that he should stay here but it is up to him. I trust that the rest of the family can accept his decisions.

After a while, Cindy and I got ready to leave. As always, I asked him what he might want me to bring when I come back. He said just one word, "*Starbucks!*" We left and went to the waiting room, feeling that Sammy and the family might want some time alone with him. After about 15 minutes, they came by where we were, having said goodbye to Daddy. They were all visibly upset, but controlled. This is truly a difficult time for each of us.

We left the hospital and I took them to the Centennial campus and showed them around. We went in Grout Chapel as well, where the Heritage Service, which I conduct, is held each Sunday. I gave them some bulletins from the past Sunday's service. We went by *Krispy Kreme* for doughnuts; I bought them a dozen for their trip home.

They eventually left our house around 4:00. I reminded them that they could stay with us when they come back. Cindy and I tried to rest after they left. I could not take a nap, even though I was very tired emotionally and mentally.

* * *

Before going to the hospital this evening, Cindy and I went to the *Rainbow Restaurant* for supper. The Christmas production at *Providence Place* is taking place; this is the final weekend. It was obvious that several people were eating before they see tonight's production. As Cindy and I were seated in a booth, I found out right away that Harold Gunsalus (the Wesleyan Church District Superintendent in Virginia) and his wife Mary were sitting behind us, eating with another couple. We spoke to each other, but I didn't tell them about Daddy. (Harold and I go back a long way. He was a mentor for me when I came to our last church, *Ramseur First Wesleyan*, as pastor in 1990. He was also on staff at *First Wesleyan* here in High Point, just as I am now. Harold took the picture that I display in my office of my Drew graduation, the one with Daddy in it. I asked him to take it for me. He and I both received our Doctor of Ministry {D. Min.} degree from Drew in 1995. The picture has been in every office or study I have had since. In the picture are Mama, Daddy, Cindy, Carol, Sammy, Edna {Cindy's aunt} and of course, me.) After the meal, I told Harold about Daddy's cancer. He was very encouraged about the spiritual report that I gave and promised me that he would pray.

We went by *Starbucks* and got coffee for both Daddy and me, Christmas blend, tall. I put sugar and creamer in his and put both in a holder. We took it to him so we could drink it together. The moment I walked in the door, the phone rang; I guessed that it was David. I sat down the coffee and handed the phone to Daddy. He told David that I had just brought him his *Starbucks* coffee. They talked while Cindy and I sat down and conversed quietly. After he was finished, Daddy said that David wanted to talk to me, so I took the phone. David told me that he was better today after the shock of yesterday. He asked me if there was any news to report. There is none. He also asked me about Carol. I told him that I spoke with her yesterday. She was originally coming Saturday, but it might be Sunday; I wasn't sure. He plans to come Sunday by himself. He and Lynda plan to come the following weekend also, arriving late Saturday evening and leaving Sunday.

Daddy had cheese toast and chicken and rice for supper. He drank almost all of the coffee and said, "Good coffee." He seemed to enjoy having some. He compared it to *Gevalia* coffee, declaring, "One cup of good coffee is better than 10 cups of bad coffee."

We talked about a lot of things. He ate all of his supper once again. Sammy called and said they made it home safely. While he didn't want to upset Daddy, he told me privately that Vada cried all the way home. I told him that I would be praying for the entire family.

Daddy and I talked about everything from Jamestown, Virginia, which he last visited in 1937 with Frankie Holden (his sister Ruby's husband), to our time at Drew University in Madison, NJ when I graduated with my doctorate. We ate in a "train" car restaurant that night, and every one of us got tickled at Sammy's stomach rumbling. We laughed about it again as we remembered the occasion. He told me about the 180 mph train from England to France that goes under the English Channel. He rode it on one of his trips to England.

He also said that our relationship with God is of first importance and then our relationship with our family. He was very sober, but smiled as he talked. I only wish that I had time to hear everything he needs to share. It is hard to make up in a few days, however, what is missed in a lifetime.

Tears were shed by both of us. He did remark, yet again, how God has worked things out exactly as they should be. He feels good in his spirit, though he is in physical pain. He wiped his eyes several times...so did I.

I left him in a good mood. The last thing he said was, "I love you both." I love him also. He knows that we will be together again. We have talked about it several times; of that we *both* are sure.

CHAPTER 12

SATURDAY, DECEMBER 11

Signed, Sealed and Delivered

Carol called while Cindy and I were waiting for our lunch at the *Golden Corral* in High Point. I had left a message on her cell phone voice mail earlier. She said she got home late last night from Tennessee and plans to come see Daddy tomorrow. She asked me how everything was going. I really didn't have any more news. She said she was going to call Daddy shortly. I told her to tell him that I would be by to see him in a little while.

I left Cindy at *Oak Hollow Mall* in High Point so she could do some desperately needed Christmas shopping while I went to visit Daddy. He was eating his lunch as I arrived, but seemed somewhat despondent. I asked how he was doing. He said he had had a rough morning. He didn't ask for his pain medicine early enough and went through a period of extreme discomfort while they did the necessary things to get him ready for the day. I told him about getting on the Percocet around the clock as a standing order and offered to check on it for him. I asked the nurse about it. She in turn asked the doctor. They wanted to put him on OxyContin (it lasts 24 hours), but Daddy said Percocet was sufficient. He said that he wanted to remain alert as long as possible and not get on the stronger drugs until absolutely necessary. They gave him his dosage right then and said that he would be getting it every four hours from that point. He told me it was a good idea and thanked me for being there and helping to look out for him. I told him he could ask for anything he might need from the nurses or doctors. He acknowledged that but said he did not want to be a "pest." I reminded him that Dr. Williford, his oncologist, said that suffering with pain would not benefit him. He acknowledged that each doctor he has seen has said the same thing and he didn't see any need to suffer either. We both felt good about the pain management issue being taken care of for now. He understands that more, or stronger, pain medicines will probably be needed later. Right now, the primary pain is in his back. He is fairly comfortable otherwise.

He did not eat as well as he had previously, but managed to eat about one-half of his meal. As he told me earlier, he has had a rough morning. I combed his hair, moved his tray and we began to talk. He asked me to let his teeth soak for a few minutes. I took them and as they soaked, he talked. We spoke about several things, as usual, but a few things remain in my mind that I want to remember. As our conversation developed, he said that he could feel the muscles in his back relaxing. That was good, obviously.

Somehow, our conversation turned to the history of the family. While he told me several things, a few interesting points are worth noting:

Daddy's mother was Vada. Her mother was Julie, a Teachey. She had some mental problems and died in bed as a recluse.

Daddy's father was Roland; Roland's mother was Elsie. She and Roland's daddy, Elzie, lived in Rose Hill. My middle name comes from him. Daddy remembers going to see them with his parents in the summer of 1934. The children piled into the back of the truck and rode over dirt roads to Rose Hill. It ended up being an all-day trip. He said that while they had electricity in Rose Hill at that time, it was still fairly uncommon. It was turned on early in the morning and stayed on until 9:00 at night. Elsie's maiden name was Dail. She was a woman of great faith who developed a cancer on her left hand. He remembers seeing her hand lying on the sheet. She said that God would provide and refused to see a doctor. Eventually, she died from cancer.

He told me about the town of "Paisley." It was located across highway 41 from the "Pink Supper House." (The Pink Supper House, which still exists, is a large pink building near Daddy's "home place" used to serve pork barbeque on Saturday nights. The funds raised from the meals support the Ruritans and other charitable endeavors. It is a community institution.) Paisley had a post office and road that actually ran from behind Uncle R. C.'s all the way to Chinquapin. He commented that there were probably not that many people who would remember it, but for him it was basically his entire world as he grew up.

We talked about the origin of Rose Hill. Highway 117 runs from there to Goldsboro and generally follows the railroad. Back years ago, most major roads followed the railroad. At one point the road literally went through a patch of roses in someone's driveway. The name "Rose Hill" caught on. Some actually referred to Rose Hill as "Rosemary." South of there, near the quarry, was actually known by some, years ago, as Rosemary.

There were five Cavanaugh brothers who married five sisters from another family (Hanchey)? They were double-first cousins, all five sets. Granddaddy Roland used to say that if they ever ran into someone they didn't know, simply refer to them as "Cousin." That is why they called so many people "Cousin" early in our family's history. I remember Grandma Vada calling people "Cousin."

He remembers going to the Chinquapin school as a very young boy. They had a preacher who came and shared from the Bible, doing an object lesson in the auditorium. One day, he came and shared the passage where Jesus said, "Seek and ye shall find." He had a large envelope. He called for Daddy to come up. (This was in 1934 during the mid-depression era.) He told Daddy to open the envelope. He did, and found another one inside. This went on for five envelopes, until in the end he found the last envelope with a $1 bill inside. This was "big money" back then. Daddy's eyes became moist as he finished the story. I told him that when we seek Jesus we do indeed find him. He said he never forgot that object lesson and what it represented.

I got up and brushed his teeth with toothpaste, dried them and put them back in his mouth. He asked me how many pages I have written up to this point. I told him about 30 or so. He said, "Hopefully, someone will find it interesting someday." I told him this journal would become one of the most cherished possessions that I own.

* * *

I went back at supper and took Daddy an original glazed doughnut from *Krispy Kreme*, along with a small "rich" blend coffee. I also took a coffee and drank it while he ate his supper comprised of roast pork, cabbage, bread and fruit cocktail; his appetite had returned. He said he had his pain medicine, Percocet, about 30 minutes earlier. It obviously makes him more comfortable. We talked.

He commented about Mr. Lowry hanging in there with David. I felt like it was a good time to ask him about the future. He filled me in on some details about his estate, including telling me that David is the executor. Our conversation soon moved to another subject so I did not question him about it further. The way his estate is settled is up to Daddy. Once again, all I want from him is the assurance that he is ready to go to heaven and I have that. I also told him that the time we have together is worth more than anything he might leave me. I have a peace about it all.

"Jesus, help me trust David and the others, and keep my mind focused on 'things above and not the things of this world.'"

I commented to Daddy that in 100 years, the only thing any of us will leave is our influence. He emphasized that everything is in order and to be divided five ways. The appropriate legal documents are in a manila envelope, and the lawyer has it all. David knows what to do when Daddy dies, and all is in order, "Signed, sealed and delivered." I asked him how long his will had been ready; he said, "This year." He continued, with a serious tone, that he didn't want things to be like they were with Uncle Frank who died almost a year ago. Uncle Frank was Daddy's older brother who died with cancer.

David, Lynda, Carol and Mike are coming to visit tomorrow. As the nursing assistant came in to change his dressing, I told him that I would see him then. I also told him that I loved him. He said that he loved me as well. I left him with the nurse.

CHAPTER 13

SUNDAY, DECEMBER 12

Investigating Options

I have returned from the hospital just now. This has been a busy weekend for Daddy and all of us. David, Lynda, Carol and Mike were all here today. I went by after lunch with Cindy to visit. No one was there when I arrived. Within 10 minutes, however, David and Lynda came. Daddy has had more pain today. It was 2:00 and his lunch tray was still untouched. It was obvious that he was not hungry. Lynda and David brought a Christmas stocking for him, along with the latest issue of the *Robesonian*, the official newspaper of Robeson County and Lumberton. Lynda made the stocking herself. She operates a florist in Lumberton and is very talented working with flowers and crafts.

David and I went out near the nurses' station to see if the doctor might be paged so he and Lynda could get an update. While we waited, David told me what a difficult time he is having with everything. He remarked that he could not sleep last night after resting the previous night. Without the extreme tiredness that comes from a day of working at the drug store, it is difficult to sleep; I certainly understand that. He feels that Daddy should go back to Lumberton and that he would probably desire to do so, under the circumstances. Many people want to see him and are asking about him. I had not thought of it that way but can see the reasoning. It is not fair to deprive them the satisfaction of seeing him again. David also commented that he wasn't sure about the situation once Daddy dies, how long the store will be able to remain open legally. The argument about people missing him I understood. We approached Daddy about going back to Lumberton. He didn't act overly concerned about it, but did give David the permission to at least "Begin to investigate the options."

As our discussion was ending, Carol and Mike arrived. Carol came in, greeted everyone, and commented on Daddy not eating his lunch. We told her that there was no use; he said he didn't want to eat with so much company present.

After a good time of visiting, I started to leave. Carol and Mike went with me (I was asked by David to tell her about the potential move of Daddy back to Lumberton.) We sat down in the waiting area between 7 North, where Daddy is, and 7 South. I told her about the funeral; I will conduct it and it will be at the funeral home in Wallace with the burial at Cavenaugh's Cemetery. Carol said she would like for it to be held at our home church, *Bethel Wesleyan*, if Daddy would agree. The church is located seven miles north of Wallace. Later today, Sammy would tell me that he had asked Philip Siebbeles about having the funeral there. Philip, the pastor, told him that with so many of Daddy's family members active at the church that would not be a problem. Sammy would like to see the funeral at the church as well. Sammy, Carol, and their families attend *Bethel*. Cindy and I also call *Bethel* home.

As to the issue of moving Daddy back to Lumberton, Carol expressed opposition to it. She feels that we should once again go to Daddy and find out his wishes. (Later that evening after I left, Daddy would give Carol strong indication that he would rather not move). He did, however, still leave it to David to look into it. As Carol, Mike and I were coming out of the waiting room, we ran into Myra Snider. Myra has been a close friend for over three years now; we hit if off from day one. She is my former secretary.

We introduced everyone and I told Carol and Mike the story about when Myra went to the drug store in Lumberton on the way to visit her mother at Sunset Beach. She had hugged David, thinking *he* was my father! She left us, remarking that she was going to visit Daddy for a few minutes. I had to go, as the seniors were going to the Christmas program at *Providence Place,* and Cindy and I were going to ride with them. As I left, Carol told me that she wanted to talk to David about the move, or lack of it. While I am open to what is best, I certainly feel that Daddy's earlier statement to Sammy and me is still in force; he desires to stay where he is. I'm not aware if there are facilities in Lumberton that are equipped to provide the same level of physical or spiritual care. That possibility needs to be investigated. I will talk to David about it soon.

CHAPTER 14

MONDAY, DECEMBER 13

Potential Fallout

It is 10:20 p. m. as I sit on my couch at home and write this. It has been a very full day. I went by to see Daddy at lunch. While I was there, Dr. Tarter came by to see him. He had spoken with Carol, Daddy, Lynda, David and Mike yesterday after I left. This stop was to simply check on Daddy. Because I am a minister, I had on my clergy badge for the hospital. He immediately identified himself as a believer. He comes from Somerset, Kentucky, the grandson of a Baptist minister. He told us that his mother always thought he would be a "preacher." Early in life, he displayed the desire to be of help to other children who fell or scraped a knee. She thought it was "minister instinct," but as it turns out, it was actually "doctor instinct." He commented that Daddy was an intelligent, kind and understanding person. He also spoke about doctors being able to help with physical needs, but that the care of the soul was of primary importance. He acknowledged that both things work together in harmony. I can understand why Daddy likes him so much. He has a genuine, caring attitude and a very good bedside manner.

Before the doctor came by, I had talked with Jennifer, who left the room after informing Dr. Tarter what she and I had discussed with Daddy. She is the social worker for 7 North. Our discussion:

Daddy will probably be discharged Wednesday.

A portacath is in order.

Hospice will care for Daddy after he reaches the nursing home.

The DON (director of nursing) will need to give the okay before Daddy's portacath can be used. It is possible that its use will eventually require Daddy to move to a facility that allows the use of a portacath.

The DON at Westchester Manor is out today, but we should hear from her in the morning.

I told Dr. Tarter, after getting the okay from Daddy, that I felt we should wait for the portacath, at least until after we hear from the DON. If Daddy can go back to *Westchester Manor* without it, it could be installed later. (Dr. Tarter confirmed that Daddy could wait and come back as an outpatient later if we desired to do so.) At that time, I was thinking that the installation might be an issue. Actually, the use of it might be more of an issue than its installation. (I would later realize my misunderstanding and give the okay, if Daddy wanted it. He was on the schedule to have it installed on Tuesday morning in his right clavicle.)

Not long after the doctor left, they gave Daddy his pain medication. He said that his pain was a "four or five" on the scale of 10. He did not eat his lunch today.

* * *

Cindy and I went back later this evening to be with Daddy during his supper. He was on his back and resting when we came into the room; his supper had not arrived. The room was quiet, with a minimum of light. He was waiting for his pain medication and has had several medical personnel by this afternoon. He told me that he felt tired and he looked it as well. He was, nevertheless, pleasant. I asked him about his supper and he said that he had ordered it recently. I inquired as to what he had ordered and he said, "Meatloaf." He loves meatloaf and spaghetti. We mainly talked about the fact that the portacath would be inserted tomorrow; it is obvious that he is comfortable with the idea. We also talked about using *Bethel Wesleyan* for his funeral. He was agreeable to what-ever I felt was best. I told him I liked the idea of the church if he did, since his funeral would be a service of worship. He said that he liked the idea of having his funeral in a church.

We covered what to tell David about his not returning to Lumberton. He said that he honestly didn't feel like he was up to the trip. He hates to tell David how he feels for fear that it will upset him. He cares deeply about the feelings of David and all of us. I have learned over the last four weeks that Daddy is a genuinely caring and kind person. He does not want to hurt anyone. I told him that I would address it with David when he calls tonight, if he wanted me to do so. He said he would like for me to do that for him.

His pain medication was brought at 5:50. The nurse informed us that the machine would not give it to her any earlier. He took the pills with some water and asked me to raise him up in the bed, which I did. His supper came, but he wanted to wait to eat it later. He likes for the medications to "kick in" before he eats. He had meatloaf, creamed potatoes, green beans, grapes, a roll, tea, coffee and milk on the tray. I got it ready, but kept it covered for later. (He would eventually eat everything). While we waited for the pain medication to kick in, we talked.

David called tonight. I discovered that he was not as strong about Daddy returning to Lumberton as I thought. I told Daddy that the Lord was working in that situation and he agreed.

Ashly called and talked to Daddy as well.

Sandra, who works at the drug store, also called. Daddy told Cindy and me about Sandra's premature grandchild who weighed two pounds. He is amazed that the child has survived. He asked Sandra to say hello to a few people. He was very tearful as he spoke with her. I can tell that it is really hard for him to let go of his life's work perhaps most of all. Still, he is very strong and remains posi-tive, though very sobered. We do laugh now and then about certain things, however.

We talked again about how things will "fall out" after his death. He would like to see the store remain open if David wants to continue working at it. He said that he and David were getting things in order to see that we all would benefit from its remaining open. He originally thought that it would be sold and divided evenly. Now, however, he sees the benefit in allowing each of us children the option of keeping our shares in the store, through incorporation and receiving the dividends on a yearly basis if we choose to do so. He said that it would be "a nice check each year." I honestly am not concerned about that, although I accept whatever he sees fit to do. I'm not sure that everyone will be happy with the way things "fall out," as he says. He and I talked at length about it. I have to trust him, and David as the executor of the estate.

Cindy and I ate a grilled cheese sandwich from the snack shop downstairs while Daddy talked on the phone and ate his grapes. I took his teeth out to soak and was getting ready to leave when the phone rang again; it was Carol. I told her to give us 15 seconds, and Daddy would talk. I put the receiver down on the bedside table, went and hugged and kissed him on the cheek, as did Cindy. I told him I loved him, and he said he loved me too. He picked the phone up to talk with Carol and was smiling as we left.

I do want to note that I read the account of John Wesley's death to Daddy along with his words, "But the best of all is, God is with us." I also read a few verses from the first chapter of John. The phone rang before I finished. I plan to share the passage on Wesley at his funeral. It seems that I am more reconciled to Daddy's death than I was. He remarked tonight that it was as if everything is falling into place, as if he, each day, has the opportunity to settle one more small item. We can both see God's hand in all that is happening.

CHAPTER 15

TUESDAY, DECEMBER 14

A Rough Month

This morning I went to staff meeting at the church. Since the conference room is next to Pastor Aron's office, he stepped in and commented that he had read the email I sent out on Monday that gave an update on Daddy's prognosis. Pastor Aron is the senior pastor of our church. He informed me that he prayed for Daddy and me after he read it. He then gave me a hug as I sat at the table waiting for the others to arrive. I feel very blessed to have a staff such as this with which to work. Soon, Cher, our small group director, came in and expressed her prayers and concerns. She told me about her husband's mother in New Bern who had died several months ago. She died from lung cancer. After that, Steve, our young adult pastor, came in. He placed his hand on my shoulder and said, "It's going to be a rough month, isn't it?" At that point, I started to cry. A bit later, John, our executive pastor, had all of the staff to gather around me and pray. Aron asked Jonathan, the middle adult pastor, to lead in prayer, noting that he was aware of what we are going through. (Jonathan lost his father to cancer a few years ago.) As Jonathan prayed for Daddy, Cindy, and me, I broke down. It was as if the strain of the last several weeks finally took its toll. After the prayer, I felt better. John told me to do "whatever you need to do." He also expressed that they "are here for (me)." I am a blessed man. I ended up crying more today than any day I have yet; it seems to hit me at unexpected times.

* * *

After attending the bulk of the staff Christmas luncheon at *Canterbury's* Restaurant, I went to the hospital to see Daddy. He was lying almost completely horizontal in the bed with his eyes closed. They had planned to put the portacath in today, but we have delayed it. There is a chance it would prevent him from going back to *Westchester Manor* and familiar surroundings. Having been scheduled to have the procedure done, he did not have breakfast, nor did he have his pain medication as normal. I called for the nurse and she gave him his Percocet. We elevated him slightly. After a few minutes, his lunch arrived: spaghetti (what else)? He told me to go ahead and get it ready. He would eat after a bit, when the pain medications had begun to work. After a while, it was obvious that his pain was not improving. I asked him what the level was and he said, "A five." Though he initially declined my offer to have the nurse give him something more, I insisted and he told me I could see if we could get him something else, a "boost" as Daddy calls it. They came and gave him something through the pick line. Within 15 minutes, I could tell a major difference in his countenance and attitude. We got him up the rest of the way, elevated his head, and he began to eat.

We discussed his potential move, as well as what we may do about his pain management. I had asked to speak with Dr. Tarter earlier and eventually he came by to visit. He said that installing the portacath was a simple procedure. Daddy could come to the hospital for one night and have it done, if needed. The plan from here is, in progressive order:

First, give oral pain medications, such as Percocet.
Move on to a morphine elixir (Roxinal) after that.
Lastly, a Duragesic patch (which goes from 25-400 micrograms of pain medication and lasts 72 hours) will be prescribed.
When Daddy goes beyond 100 with the patch, we will need to consider the portacath.

I asked Daddy if that was satisfactory to him and he agreed with "Whatever you suggest, Doctor." I asked him if he thought I had done the right thing, that is, requesting that we hold off on the portacath until all of the options and issues with the nursing home are resolved. He said that he felt absolutely comfortable with whatever I thought was best, and that he was confident we had done the best that we possibly could do. I feel satisfied with the outcome as well since we now have a clear plan in place.

I had a meeting with Wendy, the admissions director at the nursing home, and the care plan nurse at 2:30. Informing him of the meeting, I left him eating his lunch.

* * *

Earlier in the day, the social worker, Jennifer, had been in contact with the nursing home about the issue of the portacath. When the DON said they would not keep Daddy if he needed to begin using it, I called the nursing home administrator and asked him if there was any way that something could be worked out. He told me that he would investigate it. Wendy had called earlier and said that she felt confident some type of compromise could be reached. I went to the nursing home after I left Daddy, meeting with Wendy, Felton (the administrator) and the care plan coordinator. We met in the staff conference room.

I told them that I was not being hard to get along with, but stressed that Daddy wanted to be at our facility if at all possible. They want him back, commenting that I was their "pastor." (Part of my responsibilities as the senior adult pastor at our church includes coordinating the chaplain services for the nursing home.) It was a very good meeting. The plan is to bring him back and proceed with his pain management as Dr. Tarter described earlier. We also talked about Medicare paying for the five to six remaining days that he has with them and then switching to *Hospice*. Medicare will pay for *Hospice*, under the "*Hospice* benefit," but we will need to pay $160 per day for the nursing home bed and food service (just as we are doing at this time to hold his bed). I told Wendy that was a good plan and paying for his room out of pocket was not an issue.

* * *

Feeling satisfied about the future plans for Daddy, I took some items to his room from the hospital, in anticipation of his release Wednesday. As I made my way to his room, several people, both employees and residents, asked about him. They were all concerned and are looking forward to having him back. To say that he has made a positive impact on all of them, I believe, is an understatement.

When I arrived back at the office, I received a call from the hospital social worker. She gave me the name of Margie. I called Margie at *Hospice*. Their offices are located across the street from the nursing home. I shared with her the plans as outlined above, and she said that everything was in order for them to step in at the appropriate time. She also discouraged the use of the portacath/morphine pump unless it becomes absolutely necessary. Most of her patients are homebound and a portacath is not an option. A trained nurse is needed to care for it, hence the nursing home's reluctance to accept it. Ninety-five percent of the cancer patients she has worked with do very well with the patch. (I found out from Daddy that Uncle Frank was on the 25 mcg. patch at the time of his death.) His pain was controlled well with that. She said that 400 is *very* strong and almost always adequate. Morphine can also be given with a dropper in the person's cheek if they cannot swallow, yet need more pain relief than the patch provides. Therefore, she was confident that his pain could be managed without the pump. He should be able to die at the nursing home peacefully, we hope.

Hospice would come by twice a week and check Daddy over "from head to foot," she said. They have a nurse on call 24/7, and we can address all questions to their organization. As a pastor, I feel very confident that they can do what needs to be done, having worked with them in the past.

* * *

Cindy and I went back to the hospital for Daddy's supper. He was lying completely down and had received his pain medication about an hour before we arrived. We got him situated for supper (barbeque chicken sandwich, salad, fruit cocktail, milk and coffee). David called as Daddy started eating. I asked Daddy if I could fill him in on the plans for his care (while he ate and listened). He said that was fine. After talking with Daddy and myself, I think everyone is satisfied.

As we talked, it became evident that Daddy is much more comfortable tonight than this afternoon. His evenings are typically better than his mornings or lunch times.

Mr. Lowry called to talk with Daddy. A lady from Lumberton also called. (She jokingly told me that Daddy was her "boyfriend".) Daddy was very talkative and animated. I could tell that he feels better. Harold also called and asked me for the nursing home address for Daddy. He wants to send a card and a picture of his 8-month-old son. With all of the calls, it took Daddy a while to finish his meal, but he enjoyed it.

After his meal was over and the calls stopped, I asked him if I might read some scripture. I told him that I did not want to be "preachy." He assured me that he does not tire of my reading to him and that he wants to hear all that he can. I read from John 3 and Philippians 2. I talked with him about the verses and their significance. He mentioned the verses about the Good Shepherd. He said that each time he ate a meal at *The Good Shepherd Home* at Lake Waccamaw (a home for alcoholics where he stayed in 1972), he noticed the picture over the tables. It referenced the verse and said "The Good Shepherd." I told him it was also in John. I found John 10 and read several verses, including the ones about the Good Shepherd. He talked again about what a blessed man that he is.

I collected his "blue blanket," which he has had from day one, and got his teeth out to soak. I held his hand and we had a prayer, asking for God's strength for him and all of the family in the days ahead. *We will surely need it.*

He asked me to turn off all of his lights. His TV had been on *UNC*, the PBS station, and turned down low. An archeological show was on and we turned it up some. He said the show looked "interesting." When I left, he looked very content, full and groggy. We exchanged "I love you(s)" as I left him to rest.

CHAPTER 16

WEDNESDAY, DECEMBER 15

Back (Nursing) Home Again

This morning, I received a call from Jennifer, the social worker at the hospital, stating that Daddy will be discharged. I asked her to have *Westchester Manor* call me when he gets there. She said that she would have Wendy, the admissions director, do so. I did get a call at 1:00 that he had just arrived. I was at *Burger King*, but took my time, knowing that it would take a little bit to get him settled. In the meantime, James Smith, the chaplain making hospital calls today, called and told me that Daddy had visitors at the hospital, his sister and one other person. (I would later discover that Francis and Connie, both nieces, were with Aunt Sissie.)

* * *

When I arrived at the nursing home, I found Daddy in considerable pain. He had not had lunch and didn't really want any. He told me that he had eaten a "double breakfast," including scrambled eggs among other things. (Aunt Sissie and Francis would later tell me that they were with him when he had eaten breakfast, and he did indeed eat a large one.) He had not had his pain medication since this morning. He was soon given his medications and seemed to relax. He was quite tired, and I soon left. I had talked with Carol earlier this morning and as I was about to get in my car, I heard

Jason call my name; he and Carol had just arrived. I greeted them both. Jason soon went in to see Daddy while Carol and I talked in the parking lot. After 15 minutes or so, she went in as well, and I left to go to the office. Some of my work has fallen behind.

* * *

By 5:30, I was back at the nursing home. Daddy was not sitting up and obviously uncomfortable. He managed to smile and hold a good conversation in spite of the pain. Aunt Sissie, Connie and Francis were there. Connie, from Fayetteville, had been working at the *Walgreen* on North Main here in High Point today only, leaving Aunt Sissie (her mother) and Francis (Daddy's niece from Virginia) with him at the hospital. Connie had finished and all three were in the process of leaving. I gave some directions to get out of High Point, and exchanging hugs, they left.

I asked Daddy how he felt. He said he had one Percocet at 5:30. I asked him why he had not gotten two. He said that he wasn't sure, but did not want to complain. I told him that I would check on it and get his supper ordered. He had not ordered supper at that point. I left the room and had the Certified Nursing Assistant (CNA) to order his supper. She asked me if he was on a special diet; I told her he was not. (At this point, I feel he should be allowed to eat whatever he wants.) She said she would order the "house dinner" for him. I went to talk to the nurse, Jamie, as he was administering medications on the hall. He informed me that Daddy was now on a standing order for Percocet, but one pill only. I told him that would not do, that he had been on two every four hours at the hospital, not one. He said that he would check on it. He came to the room later and said that Daddy would get the one Percocet every four hours, but could have an extra one PRN (as needed). Daddy understood that he would have to ask for the second one, at least until I could get it straightened out in the morning. His next dose would be at 7:00, when he would get two.

His dinner had arrived and I asked him if he wanted to go ahead and eat; he said, "I have to eat." I elevated him as much as I reasonably could, and he began to work on his supper. He had chicken and pinto beans. I told him that pintos were like a regional favorite in this area. He ate almost all of the chicken, but little else. I don't think he is crazy about pintos. I asked him as he ate what his pain level was and he said "Four, maybe five." I asked if he wanted the "breakthrough" pain medication (the morphine elixir, Roxinal). He said he thought he could make it until 7:00. He ate slowly and eventually drank everything. Between 6:30 and 7:00, I turned on the TV and tried to take his mind off of the pain. David called and talked for 10 minutes; that helped as well. He told me he was done, so I moved his tray out of the way and told him that I would see about Jamie; it was almost 7:10. He was considerably uncomfortable. I found Jamie; he brought Daddy his medication and gave him two Percocet. I reminded Daddy again that he would have to ask for the other pill, at least until I could get it straight. I told him about *Hospice*, and how we would have a nurse 24/7 who would help with his pain medications. While the nursing home would administer the drugs, we would work directly with *Hospice* on those issues. I have worked with *Hospice* a lot in ministry. Just as I told Daddy, their work is one of the *most* deserving that I know of support. I will feel even more comfortable when they enter the picture next week. The nursing home does a great job, but *Hospice* is the most critical element in the weeks (?) ahead. Pain management is the *main* concern, although not the only one. Remaining alert is a close second.

Sammy called just as Daddy was settling down. He talked with Daddy a few minutes, until the nurse came to check his dressing (bedsores). At that point, Daddy handed me the phone, so I went out into the hall and talked with Sammy. We actually talked for a long time. It is obvious that he accepts Daddy's wishes relative to the settlement of his estate, even though we are unclear about the full implications at this time. I felt very good about our discussion; reminding Sammy that it is absolutely critical we present a "united" front as we deal with Daddy's last days or weeks on this earth. I feel that God is working all things out, just as they should be.

By the time I went back into the room, Daddy was resting comfortably. He said that he was in virtually "no pain." He has had three Percocet since 5:30.

They came to give him some other medications, so I prepared to leave and kissed him goodnight.

I vow in my heart to never mention anything relative to what happens after his death, *unless* he mentions it to me first. This earth's material things are not a priority in my life.

I left him, however, feeling that a critical element has been addressed.

CHAPTER 17

THURSDAY, DECEMBER 16
Discretionary Funds

I went by the nursing home this morning with three items in mind that needed covering:

Check on securing a new air mattress instead of using the regular one that he now has.
Secure the standing order for Percocet, two every four hours.
Let them know that he desires as much therapy as he can tolerate. He's not sure if he will actually be up to being lifted out of bed and put into the gerry chair, but desires to do whatever he can.

I spoke with Wendy from admissions about the therapy request. She would make the necessary notations. I also spoke with Maria, the care plan coordinator, about the mattress and Percocet. I did not stop in to see Daddy, as it was quite early, before 9:00 a. m.

* * *

For lunch, I went back to the nursing home for a visit. Daddy looked rather comfortable when I got there. He did not have any lunch, so I went and asked the CNA about it. I also noted that we had to call for his supper last night. She said that she would order lunch for him and make sure that he was "on the list" to receive regular meals. I went back to the room and talked with Daddy and within a few minutes, his lunch arrived. I asked the CNA if he was "on the list" and she assured me that he was. She then questioned me about help with her gas bill that she had asked me about a while back. She had requested the financial help several days earlier. I told her that the church would give her $50, but she would need to come up with the rest. I asked how much she had and she said around $100. As she started to leave, Daddy had overheard the conversation and said "Roland, I have some discretionary funds." He told me that he would take care of the balance, around $200. He told me to bring the check Friday and fill it out to the gas company and he would sign it. He said to leave the cash in his wallet. (I have been keeping his wallet, and other personal belongings, at our house for safekeeping.) The CNA was flabbergasted. She could not believe that he would do so. As we walked out, I told her we would see to it tomorrow. When I came back in, I said to him, "Daddy, what will I do with you!" He commented that if he could make her Christmas a little brighter, then that is what we will do. He is truly a special person.

Pearl came in to visit. Her brother is across the hall from Daddy and was in a wreck 31 years ago; he has been in the facility for that entire time. As she came to Daddy's side to speak to him, he tenderly kissed her hand. She said that he deserved one back and kissed him on the cheek. She is a part of an African-American, Christian family, and very strong. She has helped me many times with the nursing home service on Wednesdays, sharing the message. She is very acquainted with grief and hardship.

After a minute or two, I followed her out to explain Daddy's prognosis. I also recounted the episode with the CNA, so that she would know the kind of man Daddy is. We talked about her plans for Christmas. I told her that our plans were uncertain, based on the present circumstances.

When I went back into the room, he was still eating. Eventually, the nurse came in to give him his Percocet. She confirmed that he was now on the two pills every four hours. He asked her about his "Duragesic patch." I had not known that he was using one at this point. She confirmed that he was on the 25 mcg. patch and he asked her to show me where it was. It is located near to his right collarbone and is very small. He was not sure they had put it on, but thought it was taken care of last night sometime. She asked him about his pain level. "Four and not too bad," he responded. It was time for his next dose. We talked about how the patch goes from 25 to 75 mcg. Daddy said he thought they went much higher. (Dr. Tarter had said that it could go up to 400 mcg.) She said she wasn't sure, but that Daddy knew more about that than she did, being a pharmacist. We chuckled.

After she exited the room, I asked him if he was okay with using the patch at this stage. He said that he was all right with it and that it seemed to help. I told him that I was glad he was getting the help that he needed.

He talked about how hard life could be, an understatement, considering his present condition. He told me of "waking up" in pants and shoes, no shirt, with a bush hook in his hand, clearing the ditch on the property of the *Good Shepherd Home* in Lake Waccamaw, NC, a rehab facility for alcoholics. It was the 10th of May, 1971 (or '72, he wasn't sure). He was not aware of how he got there. He had asked himself, "Is this what my life has come to?" He talked about accepting what life brings and being thankful for today, as his eyes moistened. He didn't need to say any more for the point was well taken.

As I prepared to leave, Peggy, who works in activities, brought his mail; he had several cards. He knew I had to leave, but asked me to read the names on the return addresses, which I did. He even had a card from Ted Parker of *Ted Parker Enterprises* in Lumberton. He owns several mobile home outlets in southeastern NC. Daddy said that he was one of his best friends and a very good customer. I told him that I would read the cards to him tonight and left them on his TV. He said he was going to eat his cake; he did not eat much of his lunch. I told him that I would see him for supper and left.

* * *

Cindy and I went back to the nursing home for Daddy's supper. As we walked down the hall, the CNA said that Daddy had eaten all of his meal and wanted me to know it. When we got to his room, he was on the phone with David and looked very well. When he finished speaking to David, he gave me the phone to speak to David as well. As I talked with David, Cindy opened Daddy's cards with my pocketknife while he read them. (He received 14 today, 10 since lunch.) He was wearing his glasses, having asked for them earlier. They have been in the drawer under the TV for a good while and when he went to the hospital he had them, but I don't believe he ever put them on while he was there.

David and I talked for about 30 minutes or so, covering everything from how special a man Daddy is, to him trying to get the store situation in place for when Daddy's death ultimately occurs. We both shed a few tears as he told me to take advantage of this time and listen to what Daddy might have to say.

Eventually I went back into the room. Daddy was okay, but obviously in some pain. I went to find out about his Percocet. He was due at 8:00, but any time after 7:00 is okay. It was not quite 7:30. The nurse said that she would bring the medicine. We also talked about the elixir that was available, as he needs it. She told me as well that the patch would not be fully effective until the three days are completed, but there are no peaks or valleys with it; once it gets going, it will be in his system as a level dose. She informed me that it does indeed go from 25 to 400 mcg. She came with the medicine in a few minutes after our discussion and asked Daddy about his pain. He said he was a little uncomfortable, so she told him about the elixir and that the Percocet is given at 8:00, 12:00, 4:00, 8:00, etc., around the clock. She also told him not to wait until he was hurting significantly before calling for the "breakthrough" medication. He did not need to hurt and it was up to him to let them know. She was very encouraging.

After she left, Daddy told me that she made him feel much better about his pain management situation. I could tell that he was more at peace than he had been before the conversation.

Scott called my cell phone, so I stepped into the hall to talk with him. He filled me in on what he has learned about the form of cancer Daddy has, "small-cell" lung cancer. He said that Daddy's type of cancer is less than 15% of all lung cancers and that it is very aggressive and eventually may move to the brain. Some who have this type of cancer can become either juvenile or violent, with symptoms much like Alzheimer's. We need to remember that if that happens, it is not Daddy, but rather the disease affecting him. Scott is coming to see Daddy tomorrow and bringing his wife Kelly, and the boys, with him.

When I went back in to see Daddy, he commented that I was a popular person on the phone. I encouraged him about Scott wanting to see him and how things are coming together based on positive relational news from both David and Scott. He started to cry and told me of a dream he had while at the hospital in Lumberton. He had told me of it before, but this is what he said:

He had a meeting in the cemetery on highway 11 near *Bethel Wesleyan Church* in Rose Hill. He was under a very large Dogwood tree having a meeting with all of us children. He told us that we needed to get along. We were all in unity.

It was a dream, but it made a tremendous impression on him. He has spoken of "our meeting on the hill" several times. I understand it is his way of referencing that everything will be all right with his children.

I handed him a tissue and he cried a bit more. Good things are happening now as a result of this illness, and our influence lives on after our death, I commented. He said that life and our existence are *not* like Shakespeare. I said, "A tragedy?" He said, "Correct." He shared a quote from one of his plays that basically says our good dies with us and goes to the grave with our bones. We talked about how our good blesses others now and does *not* end at death. He shed a few more tears.

Before I left, I told him that I needed one more thing from him and asked him if he remembered. He nodded yes and said, "I don't have Alzheimer's yet, I don't think." I asked him if he knew what I was referring to and he said "I need to sign the check for the CNA." I said, "Yes." He asked me to elevate him in the bed while he signed the check for her and told me to "Take care of it." (Although he had asked me to bring the checkbook tomorrow, I decided to get it taken care of as soon as possible.) He also signed another check to use "Just in case we need it." I assured him that I would not use it unless it was needed. I lowered him back a bit, turned off some of the lights and asked him if the TV was okay. It was on a Clint Eastwood western. He said he could "handle that" and that he might turn it to "wrestling." He smiled at saying that as I left. We had exchanged goodbyes after I lowered his bed back a bit. He was very comfortable and said earlier that he was truly a blessed man and I agree; we are blessed as well.

How often does a person have this much time to get things settled? Daddy realizes that he could have died suddenly, not able to "finish business" relationally or spiritually. This time is not only strengthening him even as his body wastes away, but it is bringing us all together. How I praise God who works all things out just as He knows best. Daddy has had time to settle business while God has freed him from the guilt of his past actions and given him a peace that he himself cannot really explain. We both know it is God's grace because we talk about that almost every day.

CHAPTER 18

FRIDAY, DECEMBER 17

I Remember It to This Day

Today has been very full and fruitful. I arrived at the nursing home for Daddy's lunch and found him sitting up with the TV on low. He looked fairly comfortable. I asked him how he felt and he said he had had a busy morning. They had changed him twice and given him a bath, plus they had changed the bandages on his bedsores. He was okay, but a bit tired, telling me that around 11:00 he was given his first morphine elixir, Roxinal. I asked him how he felt about it and he said he was good with it. He stated that he was not fuzzy from it and that it took the edge off of his pain. I inquired about his lunch. They said that it was on its way. It soon came and included a barbeque chicken sandwich, potato salad and banana pudding. I got his teeth ready and lifted him to a position in which he could eat. He began to eat and we talked. The discussions soon turned to a couple of stories from his early childhood. Before I finished hearing the first story, I went to the nurses' station on the hall and got a piece of paper; I had an ink pen. I made some notes while he talked. I mentioned the possibility of using a tape recorder, but he didn't especially want me to do so. He did say, however, that he wished he had done something like I am doing on his father's life, keeping a written record of some of the events. He agreed when I said, "We only go around once." I then took some notes while he told some stories.

He remembers riding in a "Chevrolet touring car" when he was only two or three years old. He thinks it was probably a 1928 model. Grandma Vada was driving and Daddy was so small he could hardly see out of the windows. He remembers the ball on the stickshift "being brightly colored, perhaps marble." Grandma actually taught school, to boys between 5 and 15 years of age. He said that he saw the document from the county that certified her to teach. It was in Uncle Frank's trunk, along with other items that were lost in the flood of 1999. She taught at two different schools: Northeast school (very near Northeast Pentecostal Free-Will Baptist Church at "Elbert Hanchey's place"), and the other one near the Cavenaugh Cemetery on highway 41, just south of it and on the opposite side of what is now the highway. He also told me that Uncle Charles, his oldest brother, was one of her students.

He remembers an event at school when he was in the 7th grade. The room had several desks. The "prim and proper" girls sat closest to the front in single desks, while the boys mostly sat near the back in double desks. Daddy and Elwood Fountain (from "Fountaintown," not very far from Northeast) sat at a desk together. His father ran a store in Fountaintown and Elwood always had bubblegum or candy, or "whatever he could grab as he ran out to catch the ride to school." He and Daddy were always cutting up and had something going on. The teacher "had a problem" with them, according to Daddy. Her name was Mrs. Bannerman, the stereotypical elementary school teacher with white hair and horn-rimmed glasses. Elwood told a joke to Daddy and he shared it with the girl ahead of him, and so on. Eventually the girls on the front row were laughing. Mrs. Bannerman asked Evelyn Blanchard what was funny. (Effie Brock had told the joke to Evelyn.) The story was related to her and traced back to Daddy and Elwood. Mrs. Bannerman kept them in at recess, giving them a lecture that, as Daddy said, "I remember to this day." She was not angry, but was serious as she told them they were both bright boys and that "What you put in your mind will stay there forever. It's like the Northeast River; whatever you put in at the beginning will come out somewhere. If you want to do well in life, put the right things in your *mind. If you put foolish things in your mind, it will impact all that you do." I agree that this is still good advice today.*

Sammy, Sandra, Vada and Mama came soon after Daddy had finished his lunch. They would stay until after 6:00. Mama felt that she really wanted to talk to Daddy while he was still able to understand and talk to her. For about an hour, she talked with him while the rest of us waited outside on the patio of the 100 hall. When we got back into the room, they were still talking. Both had tears in their eyes and embraced as we entered. It was a very moving scene to me and I feel certain that the others felt the same way. (Mama later told me that they talked about the four of us; both agreeing that we all turned out fine. He was sorry for what he had done and acknowledged that he had made a lot of mistakes, but could not go back and relive his life. Mama assured him that *all* of us were comfortable with him and that God's grace allowed us to put it all behind us.) I later asked if she felt satisfied and she said that she did. She will never know how much her visit meant to Daddy...or to me personally. He needs forgiveness and encouragement more than anything else during this critical time of his life.

Mama, Vada, Cindy and I went to our house a little after 5:00. I walked Odie, our dog, while they ate ham sandwiches. While we were gone, Sammy talked to Daddy alone while Daddy ate his supper. I would later ask Daddy about it. He said that he felt much better about everything relative to his children. He again mentioned his "meeting on the hill" in the cemetery, which I referenced earlier in this journal. He was obviously very grateful with the results of the day.

* * *

Scott, Kelly, Collin and Ethan came tonight. They are going to stay until Sunday evening. Sammy and his crowd left a little time after Scott arrived. Cindy and I visited with them for a bit. Kelly left with Ethan (he was obviously very tired) while Scott stayed and showed Daddy various pictures that he had brought. They were from White Lake, NC (years past) and of Scott and his family, among other things. I want to give Scott plenty of time and space with Daddy, but also want to visit with him myself while he is here. He plans to come back several more times.

I left him in Scott's care, telling Scott that I normally take Daddy's teeth out for him. As I moved near Daddy to tell him good-bye, I noticed something in his right hand. He handed it to me. It was a smooth stone with "FAITH" engraved on it. He said that Mama gave it to him. He asked me, with tears in his eyes, to put it in the drawer with his glasses; I did just that. When I left, Scott and Daddy were enjoying their visit. I will plan to join in at lunch tomorrow.

CHAPTER 19

SATURDAY, DECEMBER 18

Slowly Losing Control

Last night, Cindy and I went to bed about 11:00. Before 11:30, I think I must have been having a dream about Daddy. I do not recall what the dream was about, but I woke up thinking about him and the rest of the family: Carol, Sammy, David and Scott. I suddenly had a lump in my throat and began to silently cry as I lay there. Eventually, Cindy heard me, asking me if I was okay. After several seconds, I managed to say "I'm okay." She got me some tissue and I cried a little more. All I could think about was that Daddy was actually going to die. I have cried quite a bit, as I have noted, but this time was different. While I know that he will be, no he *is*, in God's hands, I still cannot imagine what it is going to be like when he is finally gone. However, as Paul said, "We are confident, I say, and would prefer to be away from the body and at home with the Lord" (2 Corinthians 5:8). Eventually, that one thought sustained me and I slept well the rest of the night. There are a couple of things, however, that I *hope* to do to honor his memory:

I plan to place a plaque on 7 North at the hospital in memory of Daddy, acknowledging the care that he received. They have a couple of places where they presently put them.

My goal is to run a marathon. It will be my first one and I will run it in memory of him. His name will be on my race number. I hope to have people sponsor me, with the money going to Hospice, or some type of cancer research organization. I would like to run it within two years, if possible.

Aron Willis, the Senior Pastor where I presently serve as pastor to senior adults, just called. He wanted to know where Daddy is located. I told him he was in 108 at our nursing home. He plans to go by today and visit with him. He told me to look up and know that the entire staff is praying for me. The support that I feel from him and the rest of the staff is very meaningful.

* * *

When Cindy and I arrived at the nursing home, Daddy was sitting up in bed and a bit uncomfortable; he had on his glasses. Scott and the LPN came in momentarily. She began to question Daddy about his pain. He had been very uncomfortable earlier this morning. He said it was because he was turned several times to change him, bathe him, dress his bandages, etc. He also acknowledged that he had more "general" pain and especially mentioned his abdomen. He received the morphine elixir about 11:00; it was now just after 12:00. He had his lunch tray in front of him and seemed to be easing off. The nurse reminded him that we can move up the scale on the Percocet and also that he can take more morphine if needed. There was also some discussion about the patch and we were reminded that he is only on 25 mcg. for now. He said that he was all right at this time. Scott told him that he (Daddy) is in control and that he makes his own decisions. I affirmed that I certainly agree and that Daddy and I have talked about this very point many times. As long as he is able, he will make all of his decisions. (I later told Scott, nevertheless, that Daddy needs to be reminded, and encouraged, to let them know if he needs some "breakthrough" medication, or to increase the amount(s) that he is currently taking. He is on the same level of Percocet that he has been on for at least the last four and one-half weeks.)

As we talked, Kelly and Ethan came. Daddy mulled over his lunch and we talked. At that point, he seemed more comfortable.

The following little tale was one that he said might be worth "putting into that book that you are writing," with a smile.

When Daddy worked at Wallace Drug Company, the doctor's office was upstairs. Dr. Hundley would call down the "scripts" to the drug store downstairs. A Mrs. Brinkley was given a particular prescription. The directions for it were to add a certain amount to one quart of warm water and "Use every so often." In six weeks, she called the drug store, saying that she had mixed it as prescribed, but that she could not "get it down." Daddy chuckled (though it hurt) when he told us that the prescription was for application to the skin. We all thought that was pretty funny.

Before Kelly and Ethan had come in, Betty, who used to work in laundry at the nursing home, came by to visit. She had heard that my father was in the nursing home and simply came by to say hello. Before she left, she wanted to pray. She asked us to join hands. Cindy, myself, Scott, Ethan, Kelly and Daddy joined hands and she prayed for us. Daddy was crying.

I found out also that Pastor Aron had been by, but it was right when Daddy was having the most pain. The visit was not extremely pleasant.

Around 1:30, Carol, Mike and Eric, their oldest son, came. Sandra, from the drug store, and her friend Pete also came to visit Daddy. Pete has family in Thomasville. Daddy was very glad to see her; I can tell that he thinks a lot of her. I also heard him tell her how much he appreciates what she and Mr. Lowry have done at the drug store in his absence. When Carol arrived, she, Scott, Mike, Kelly and I went into the TV area down the hall to talk. Scott expressed concerns about some things that he was seeing in Daddy before we sat down. (Cindy had taken Collin and Ethan to hear part of a Christmas concert being held in the dining hall for the residents. They were finishing as they got there, but she did get them to play *We Three Kings* for the children; they seemed to enjoy that. She came back to the TV room with them as we sat down to talk.) Based on Scott's observations, the following items were discussed. (Scott has expertise with oncology patients and can obviously see things that I would miss. As he and I would later discuss, I care more for the soul, he for the body. While he downplayed my reference to him being a "professional," I still respect his experience and observations very much.)

Daddy has developed a cough (it reminds me of Sunday two weeks ago when he developed pneumonia).

He has trouble coughing; it is painful. He has acknowledged having pain in his diaphragm. When he can cough, he doesn't really manage to cough up much.

His breathing today is shallow. While not to the point of my noticing, Scott feels that he is in more pain than he admits (he did admit this morning, reluctantly, that his pain was a seven, the highest he has said since being here over the last month). Being in pain would cause him to not breath as deeply. Scott also noted that he never takes a deep, "catch-up breath," nor does he sigh.

We know that Daddy is reluctant to take the extra pain medication. I will feel better, though I certainly have high regard for our nursing home, when *Hospice* comes in a day or two. They will monitor him closely and will be available 24/7. They will also be of great help with his pain management issues. Cindy and I soon left, planning to come back this evening around supper.

* * *

While I was writing the last paragraph (we are still home at just before 5:00 p. m.), Carol called from *Oak Hollow Mall*. She, Mike, Eric and Scott are there so Daddy can get some much-needed rest. She relayed the following to me:

Daddy has been showing more symptoms of pain, verbalizing it (Oh!) and clinching his fists. Carol asked him about his pain and he said that he was okay. Scott pressed the issue and the nurse brought him the morphine elixir. Before taking it, Daddy asked Scott if he should. Scott affirmed that it would be good to take it. Daddy was crying as he took it. I believe I am seeing in Daddy what I have seen in other cancer patients that I have seen die over these last 16 plus years of ministry. Daddy is scared, not of death perhaps, but of the dying process. He wants to have as much control as he possibly can for as long as he can, as I mentioned above, several days ago. I wonder too if he feels that with every step into stronger pain medication, he is closer to that "point of no return," a point where he will not be as alert as he desires, a point where he finally loses conscious contact with us? He wants so much to be able to talk to us…and other friends that he has, many made while here in High Point. I'm wondering, but do not know for certain, if he realizes that time is closer?

Carol said that Scott remarked that he feared Daddy would die from pneumonia before the actual cancer takes his life. I told Cindy the same thing as we were leaving the nursing home earlier today. He now is on Percocet, the same dosage with which he began, the patch and the morphine elixir. I honestly feel that he will resist a deeper progression into pain management, if he can physically do so, based on my thoughts above.

As we age, we lose control of so many things. Daddy is slowly losing control of everything. I am sure it is scary, though I obviously do not know. He has lost control of the bodily functions of elimination, his ability to be ambulatory, the ability to do personal grooming and now the ability to control his pain or even remain as "alert as (he) can for as long as (he) can." I am leaving him even more in God's hands than ever before. "God, your grace is sufficient." Daddy and I have talked about it quite a bit; now we must fully lean on it.

Carol asked me if I thought Ashly should come before next weekend, Christmas. I honestly do not know. While I think that Daddy will almost certainly be alive then, I do not know if his pain and pain management will allow him to be as alert as I know that he wants to be. I have a feeling that he will remain alert, if at all possible, until he sees his last two grandchildren, Austin and Ashly.

Carol and I do not feel that Daddy can have extended time left, maybe a month, probably less.

I want to serve him communion while I still have the opportunity. He told me two days ago that the last time he took it was at the Notre Dame Cathedral in Paris a few years back. I would like the privilege of partaking together with him, if God so sees fit. I will try to do that this week.

* * *

Cindy and I went back to be with Daddy after being home for a while. Daddy was visiting with Henry Cavenaugh (my second cousin), his wife Kathryn and their one-year old daughter, Eliza. They adopted her about 13 months ago as an infant. Lynda met us at the door by the TV room. She and David had arrived about 4:00. I thought they were coming Sunday, but they were able to come this afternoon. David was sitting in the chair by Daddy's bed when we entered, talking with him. The baby was running around, enjoying the atmosphere and the attention.

Daddy was working on supper, and his appetite seemed to be pretty good considering the kind of day that he has had. I greeted him and asked him about his pain; he said that it was under control. He did look rather relaxed when compared to earlier today. We all talked and just enjoyed being together. I asked him if he wanted some coffee and he answered in the affirmative. David and Lynda went with me to the food preparation room near the TV area. The coffee was not made, but we stood near the 100 hall nurses' station and talked. I filled David in on Daddy's day, including the "issues" with his pain. None of us want him to suffer needlessly. I also told him that Daddy had another small cough and that I wondered, as did Scott, if pneumonia might take his life before the cancer does. Eventually, we made our way back to the room. Before long, Carol and Scott came into the room. She asked Daddy about his pain and he said he was okay. Henry had just left, offering prayer and a promise to come back. He also told Daddy that I had informed him about his spiritual surrender. With tears in his eyes, Daddy confirmed that he has turned everything over to God. I took his right hand in mine as he spoke.

While we were all there, after Henry and Kathryn had left, Daddy looked at a couple of cards he had received today. They were both from people in Lumberton. He also opened a gift given to him by Marlena, the daughter of a resident on Daddy's hall. The whole family is Lumbee and originally from Lumberton, having moved here several years ago. She has been very kind to Daddy and he has come to love and appreciate her. The gift was a ceramic "Christmas scene" drug store. It had "Williams' Pharmacy" on the building, but Marlena had a friend to skillfully paint "Sam's Pharmacy" over it. She told me earlier that they were going to do so. She is so very thoughtful. She also gave him a set of figurines that go with it, including two signposts. The two items were beautifully wrapped. The ornaments that were attached to the bows on the gifts were placed on the small Christmas tree on his closet, the one David and Lynda brought the Sunday that Daddy went to the hospital with pneumonia. The time of unwrapping the gifts was very enjoyable to Daddy. I can tell that even though the visits are tiresome, he is so thrilled to have so many expressions of love and caring given to him during this time. After a while, he was obviously in pain yet again.

I went down to the nurses' station and asked them if he could have his Percocet. (He gave me the "okay" to tell them that he was calling for the morphine elixir.) His nurse said both would be taken to him right away. (It was about 7:15.) He can have the Percocet at 7 or 8, 11 or 12, and 3 or 4 around the clock, with the morphine given as needed or as he requests it. She mentioned the possibility of bumping his patch from 25 to 50 on Monday, after she calls the doctor. She took the medicine to Daddy, i. e., Percocet, morphine and a new 25 mcg. patch. I found out later that he told her to wait on changing the 25 to a 50 while I was at the nurses' station.

As Daddy was receiving his medicine, Harold had called the nurses' station, and I stepped out into the hall to take the call. He had misplaced Daddy's phone number. Harold is the gentleman that Daddy helped move through the "12 steps," from addiction to pharmacy school. He wants to come and visit on Christmas, bringing his wife and young son; he works in Fayetteville. We talked for a while and I was able to give him Daddy's phone number again. He said that he would call tomorrow after he gets out of church. I said that Daddy was in a good bit of pain at the moment, but assured him that I would tell Daddy that he plans to come with his family on Christmas. I know Daddy will be pleased. Harold means a great deal to Daddy; he has expressed it to me several times over the last few weeks. Just as he has told me how proud he is of all of his children, he has also expressed how proud he is of Harold and the contribution he is making to the lives of others.

* * *

I went back to Daddy's room and visited with him, Carol, David, Lynda and Scott. Others present, though not in the room, included Mike, Eric and Cindy. About 8:30, I said goodbye and told Daddy that I would see him tomorrow afternoon as soon as I could. He told me that I needed to take care of his teeth before I left (like I know how better than anyone else present!). I told him that I would leave "directions with Scott," hugged and kissed him, and left the room. After speaking to most of the ones there, Cindy and I left to go prepare the chapel on the Centennial campus for services tomorrow.

* * *

Cindy and I went to Grout chapel to get it ready for tomorrow. I secured the portable communion set to use when Daddy feels up to it and the time is appropriate. I am also feeling a sudden urge to keep the funeral folder on Daddy handy. I am not sure when I will need to be prepared. I would much rather get it almost ready now. I do not want to have to deal with it before the visitation or funeral, whenever that time comes. *May God help Daddy and us all. This is not going to be easy...*

A very early photograph of my father and mother
from about 1948

Daddy working behind the counter at the drug store
in Rose Hill during the 1960s

All of my father's children (me, Sammy, Scott, Carol and David) pose with my brother Delwood in this 1982 photograph.

Ashly and Daddy at Christmas,
approximately 1982

Mama and Daddy with me at my graduation from
Southern Wesleyan University in 1985

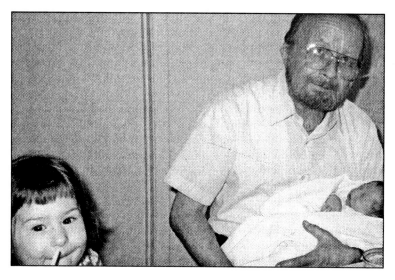

Daddy welcomes yet another grandchild into the world, Austin,
as Vada looks on in this 1987 photograph.

Daddy and his older brother Frank were not just brothers;
they were good friends as well.

My father was a lover of books. Here, he finds something to read
during our family's first summer trip to White Lake, NC.
Our extended family went to the lake for many years without
a break during the 1980s and '90s.

I was blessed to have several people attend the graduation ceremonies
when I received my Doctor of Ministry (D. Min.) degree
from Drew University in 1995. Present were Sammy, Mama, Carol,
Cindy, Cindy's Aunt Edna, Daddy, and of course, me.

Daddy is all smiles in this photograph from White Lake.
Sammy and Scott join him.

CHAPTER 20

SUNDAY, DECEMBER 19

The Most Blessed Man on Earth

I called Daddy at 12:30 as Cindy and I ate lunch. He took a while to get to the phone. I was almost ready to hang up when he finally answered it. He said that he had been sleeping soundly, that his lunch was there and that he told them that I would help feed him when I arrived. He told them that he was sure I was going to come by later. He also said that Scott had left around 11:30. I tried to call Scott after I hung up with Daddy, but he did not answer his cell phone.

* * *

It was 1:30 or so when Cindy and I arrived at Daddy's room. He was sitting up in the bed, but not high enough to eat, watching *Smokey and the Bandit* on TV. I commented, in my best southern drawl, that it was a real "redneck movie." He said, "Precisely." We both agreed that it is very funny.

I questioned him about his pain; he told me that he did not have any. I asked him about his medications and he said that they were on schedule. He informed me that he had morphine about 11:00 or so and he had been in quite a bit of pain earlier in the morning. When I asked if there was anything else to mention about his pain or medications, he said "No more." At that time Scott called, saying that he was sorry that he had to leave without seeing me today. I told him that I understood completely and thanked him for coming, reminding him that our house was available when he comes again. He said that he was present when they brought Daddy's morphine and they gave him the five units (he had taken two or three before, although five was available to him). Daddy did not tell me that five units was now the normal dosage. Scott and I talked a bit about how this time was special to us both, since we have never really lived with Daddy. He said he might be back on Christmas, and that he would probably come alone, taking me up on the offer to stay at our house in Thomasville. I told him that I loved him; he said that he loved me and to tell Daddy the same. He would see him soon. I told Daddy as soon as I hung up the phone.

Momentarily, the nurse who works weekends came in to see about Daddy's pain. He told her it was probably about a "One." She said that she had come in earlier and the two of them had talked. She listened to Daddy and he had listened to her. (She has a disabled child at home.) She said that they both talked and cried. She bragged on Daddy being such a good listener; his eyes moistened at her kind words.

She said that Daddy might need to have his standing order for morphine moved from every four hours, as needed, to every two hours as needed. I asked Daddy if it was okay if they checked with the doctor tomorrow about it. He said that was okay. "I have come to the realization that I do not need to hurt." I agreed and reminded him that all he had to do was ask for the morphine. We thanked the nurse as she left.

Scott had left two cards with Daddy. By this time, his lunch was over. (He ate every bit of it). I asked if he wanted to look at the cards, and he informed me that he was given instructions to look at them after Scott had left. I opened both cards and handed them to him; one was funny, while the other one was serious and spoke about the importance of faith. Scott had written a very moving note in the second card. After reading them, Daddy handed them to me. (He wanted Cindy and me to see them.) He had tears in his eyes as he said, "I don't feel like I deserve all of this." I know what he means. He has seen the overwhelming shower of support and love that his situation has generated. I told him that it was a gift of God's grace; none of us deserve to be so blessed. With tears running down his face, he said, "I am the most blessed man on earth." I assured him that we are all blessed for knowing him.

He began to talk about how proud he was of all of the children. He said many kind words about Scott, especially. He also said that he was beginning to understand why I chose to go into the ministry. I told him that I did not really choose it as much as it (God) chose me. He simply nodded his head in affirmation. At this point, I asked him if he would like some coffee and he said that he would, so we had some brought. The nurse came with it in a little while. She knows exactly how he likes it: one sugar only, with no cream or artificial sweetener. Before he had a chance to really drink it, they came to turn him on his side; they try to turn him every two hours because of the bedsores. I prepared to go and told him that I would plan to be back for supper and left.

* * *

I went back to see him for supper, arriving very close to 6:00. He was in an almost flat position with the TV on low volume and his tray nearby, untouched. He said that they had offered to get it ready earlier, but he told them that he thought I would soon be by to help him. He had me to go tell them that I would get it ready for him, which I did. The nurse came and took the plate to warm it up and she also brought some ice for his tea. His meal consisted of a slice of roast pork, flat green beans, yam patties, two teas, water and bread. (He told me that yams are from Puerto Rico, while sweet potatoes are what he grew up with in the southeastern part of the state. I asked him what the difference was and he wasn't exactly sure. We also talked about Brunswick County and Tabor City. He mentioned the "Yam Festival" in Tabor City.) I put butter on the bread and went to get some vinegar for the meat. He said that made it "barbeque." That was all they had to season with, other than salt, pepper and hot peppers when he was growing up. He likes vinegar on most anything; so do I.

As he ate, we talked a while. He told me that Harold had called about 4:00, but didn't sound like he felt well, maybe a head cold.

Daddy wasn't sure if he said he was coming on Christmas Eve or Christmas day. Carol called as well and said that Scott had run into heavy snow near Asheville, and she wasn't sure if they were home yet. She would let me know if they did not make it safely home.

David called as Daddy neared the end of his supper. Part of the discussion included the following tidbits:

He offered to bring Daddy some banana Moon Pies. (Daddy ate them fairly often when he was still in his apartment in Lumberton.)

Daddy gave me a brief history lesson on the Moon Pie (he <u>literally</u> knows about a <u>lot</u> of stuff). The Moon Pie is almost 90 years old. (He also got into the history of Pepsi, which time does not permit me to recite. The description was fairly detailed. Again, he knows about a lot of subjects. <u>Everything</u> is interesting to him, particularly history.)

He told David, and I quote here, "If I had a Moon Pie, I'd eat it right now; just don't bring me 12."

Moon Pies (bigger than the ones we have now) were sold at Chinquapin High School while Daddy was a student there in the 1940's, but he was never able to afford one. They were five cents.

Chinquapin was originally called "Scuffletown" before there was a post office. He said that people drank beer on the weekends and would often get into "scuffles." He said it was "similar to the situation in Jacksonville." (The scuffles are what he was referring to I think.)

He closed his conversation by telling David (redundantly), "Having children to discuss important issues and unimportant issues with is the most important." The lighthearted setting became more somber as his face became covered with tears yet again.

We talked some after he hung up with David. I asked him if he wanted some coffee; he did, as usual. I went to get each of us a cup from the break room behind the nurses' station on his hall. When I returned, we opened the Danish cookies that David and Lynda had brought. I ate two cookies, but he did not feel that he could "eat another bite." He was becoming more uncomfortable. Did he want me to call for his pain medication? He said to go and tell them. I asked him if he wanted the morphine as well to which he responded, "I better."

In a few minutes, she brought the Percocet and the morphine. The morphine is a bluish color; Daddy says that it is tasteless. I offered him water with which to wash it down, but he declined. The nurse explained, as he held the morphine in his mouth, that it works best to let it set under the tongue for a while and to resist drinking anything for a bit after it was taken. After Daddy swallowed it, the three of us talked together for a few minutes.

She bragged on Daddy and his good attitude. We talked about the importance that compassion plays in the healthcare profession...and in life in general. Daddy cried as I described him as "an old-fashioned, caring pharmacist." He remarked that so many today are "just in it for the money." She said that she was going to cry if she didn't leave, asked if he needed anything, and left.

A very short time later, the CNA came by to change his dressings. Before she got busy, I hugged him, kissed his neck and told him that I loved him. He said, "I love you, son." I told him that I would see him at lunch the next day and, gathering my coat, left him to rest. I could tell that the morphine had helped him to relax. Today has been a good day for him.

CHAPTER 21

MONDAY, DECEMBER 20

Two Major Issues

The staff meeting at the church ended at 11:45. I got to the nursing home at about 12:15. Daddy was partially elevated with his lunch on the bedside table; he had not touched it. He seemed to be uncomfortable and admitted that he was having pain in his abdomen at that time. He informed me that he had taken five units of morphine around 9:30 and was already hurting again. I told him that we are planning to check on getting his dosage moved from every four hours as needed, to every two hours as needed; he was agreeable to that. When I questioned him about me checking on it, he told me to have them bring the morphine as soon as possible. He had eaten a late breakfast. (They allowed him to sleep after his morphine dose. He was so restful after a time of significant pain this morning.) I went to speak to Maria, the care plan nurse, about bumping up his morphine frequency if he requested it. She confirmed that was not a problem. We also talked about bringing *Hospice* in soon. She explained that *Hospice* covers many issues related to the "end of life." We talked about continuing to manage his pain without *Hospice* for a few more days, but I told her that we wanted to get them involved more quickly if needed. She said to be in touch with her in the next couple of days and then went to see if the morphine increase could be taken care of immediately. She said it would only take a few minutes.

Returning to his room, I told Daddy what Maria and I had discussed; he was agreeable to it all. We talked about the two major issues that is now facing. (I asked him if these were the two major issues and he agreed.)

Pain management is a concern.
"To remain as alert as I can, for as long as I can," is his other chief desire.

I asked him if he was concerned about *Hospice* coming in, (from the pain medications angle), and he acknowledged, "Yes." I told him that *Hospice* was not simply to keep him pain-free "at all costs," but that they would work with us and help manage the medications, even making recommendations to help him remain "as alert as you can for as long as you can." I suggested that I might call them again soon and asked him if that was okay. He trusted me to do whatever was best, telling me that he was glad to have me as his "advocate."

As we talked, he began to look more visibly relaxed. Moving himself in the bed by use of his arms had made him more comfortable, he informed me. He said he wasn't really in pain like earlier and that it was mainly an "ache" in his abdomen from being bent in the bed, but not an acute pain. He was aware that something else was going on in his abdomen as well, but said that he wasn't concerned about it. He stated that he really did not want to know what was going on at this point. He is apparently suspicious that the cancer has spread, though he clearly does not want to dwell on that possibility.

We began to talk about other things and I made a few notes.

Henry Berry Lowry was an Indian renegade in the Lumberton area during and after the Civil War. He was a "Robin Hood type."
He was from the Pembroke area and drove both the Union and Confederate governments crazy, plundering and burning in order to gain back for the Lumbees what was rightfully theirs already.
He just escaped several times by the "hair of his head" and has become a legend of sorts among the Lumbees.
No one really knows what happened to him. Was he killed? Some say he escaped to the North. No one knows for certain.

I asked him again what the name of the book was that tells the "probable" story of the Lumbee Indians and their connection to the Lost Colony and Ocracoke on the Outer Banks of North Carolina. He said that it was written by a Pembroke University history professor by the name of Adolph Dail in the 1960s. Pembroke is very close to Lumberton. The name of the book is *The Only Land I Know*. I told him that I wanted to look up H. B. Lowry and the book on the Internet. He was confident that I would find a lot of information there.

They eventually brought his Percocet and morphine and he took them both, even though he was not in intense pain at the time. He was almost ready to eat. The CNA had warmed his plate and brought him fresh ice water in the bedside pitcher. She checked his blood pressure as he got ready to eat; it was 135/68. His temperature was 98.7. After the morphine had time to settle (about 10 minutes), he began to eat. I told him that I would take care of the gas bill for the CNA and also call *Hospice*.

As I prepared to leave, he continued to try to eat. He promised that he would do his best to eat at least one-half of it and he would give me a "full report" when I returned around supper. I got my coat and gloves (it was 8 degrees this morning) and left.

I can tell that Daddy's condition is gradually getting worse. I told him today that I wanted to help him "finish strong." He continues to express his faith in Christ, though he told me today that it is hard to let go. I tearfully said that I want him to hang on as long as he can, but to feel free to let go when the time comes, but not yet. He knows that time is coming, but he wants to delay it as long as he possibly can; I can certainly understand that. Today had its times of sadness, but he still continues to be as upbeat as possible. I have never seen anyone with as good an attitude as he has. He continues to speak of God's peace that he has. I told him that I was praying for that peace to fill his heart during these days and that we all would truly find God's grace sufficient. That made him cry, though he also finds encouragement in the thought.

* * *

When I arrived at the nursing home for Daddy's supper, the hall nurse greeted me, laughing. She said that Daddy was waiting for me. She then put her head near his door and asked him if he wanted her to tell me what he had told her. He said to tell it, with a smile on his face. She told me that the reason he was not eating his supper, other than a bowl of soup that he had already eaten, was because he was waiting for me to come and warm the rest of it for him. There is a room attached to the TV area on the 100 hall which is used for a break room of sorts. It has coffee, condiments, creamer and a microwave that we can use as needed or desired. I told her, for his benefit, that I think we are spoiling him. He chuckled and said that he was already spoiled. The nurse and Daddy both thought this little exchange was the funniest thing. Daddy was feeling good, obviously, and was not in pain at this point.

Before I proceeded to get his dinner tray situated, I asked him about his pain. He said that he actually felt very comfortable and was without pain. He had not had morphine since the dose received earlier today, just before I left. I think the rest and constant turning helps keep him from being in as much pain.

We took a look at what was under the lid of his tray. He had a turkey sandwich, with all of the trimmings. (He said that it was a "very good" sandwich as he gradually ate it.) We joked about it not needing to be warmed. He said that he didn't even know what it was, but that he "liked the attention," with a smile. I like to give it to him as well. With all that he continues to face, I feel privileged to give him all of the attention that I can. I think we both understand how rare these moments are eventually going to become.

During supper and after, Daddy had several calls. He heard from:

David: Everything was fine. Daddy and I both talked to David. He and Daddy discussed the future of the business and Daddy would like for the drug store to stay open, if all of us would want that. I can tell that it would be a big boost for him if he knew that the business would continue through us, his children, after his death. He talked with me after he and David finished their conversation. He said that David was working hard to get the store incorporated in the names of all of us. When Daddy dies, after incorporation, the business could remain open, as long as we want that to be the case. He said they hoped to have the legal aspects ironed out before Christmas. I assured Daddy that I certainly would not sell my portion, but would rather receive the yearly dividend. I wasn't sure, but told him that I thought the others would feel the same way. David wants to keep it open; Daddy feels confident of that.

Carol: I spoke with her and she has had a hard day. She said that she was mainly concerned about Daddy being afraid of this dying process. I assured her that this was natural. We both agreed that we felt confident that Daddy is going to heaven. She seemed to feel better after we talked. (Today has actually been a good day for Daddy and even me.) Tomorrow might be different. Carol spoke with Daddy for a few minutes after I spoke with her.

Harold: He is coming Christmas and bringing his family.

Sandra, from the store: Daddy talked with her and continues to express his appreciation for what she has done and will continue to do for David and the store.

Mr. Lowry, from the store: Daddy really enjoyed his call and actually spoke to both Mr. and Mrs. Lowry. He and Mr. Lowry really did some laughing. He did want to ask him his opinion on the incorporation idea. Evidently, Mr. Lowry was affirmative and made the following statement (which Daddy relayed to me as Mr. Lowry spoke) to put "into that book": "Two heads are better than one, even if one has sawdust instead of brains."

After all of the calls, Daddy was looking a bit tired. I am so thankful that he has friends, people to encourage him and laugh with him. We talked about how wonderful all of the activity surrounding him is. He said that he actually "enjoys it, but enjoy is relative." I know exactly what he means. I told him that I took care of the gas bill for the CNA. He commented that he was glad it was done and that at least her Christmas will be warm. His care for other people is not short of amazing. These last several weeks have enabled me to see a side of him that I have never known and I thank God for it.

He and I had spoken earlier about when to get *Hospice* involved. He has agreed that we might want to go ahead and bring them in. I reminded him that *Hospice* does more than pain management alone. They also talk about and lead both the patient and the family, through various "end of life" issues. I also told David and Carol about the decision on the phone. They are agreeable to whatever Daddy thinks is best. I told Daddy that I would call them again tomorrow with an update. He said that was okay by him.

His being tired (from talking!), I helped get him settled back in bed. I straightened his pillow, gave him some water, removed his teeth to soak and kissed him goodbye. As usual, he told Cindy and me that he loves us and we told him that we love him also. I asked if he wanted morphine (if they brought his medications soon), but he said that his pain was under control. With that, we told him goodbye, promising to come back tomorrow.

Before we actually walked out of the room, I asked him if there was anything he wanted. He mentioned an Italian sub from *Subway*. Cindy asked him what he liked on it, what David typically ordered on it for him, and he said, "I'm not sure." She asked if he liked white bread or wheat to which he said, "I'm not sure." We discussed the various condiments for it and his answer was always the same, "I'm not sure." Needless to say, it got pretty funny as it went on and we all three laughed. I eventually told him that we would all eat an Italian sub together for Christmas Eve; that pleased him.

Finally, I asked if I might serve him communion in the near future. He said, as his eyes glistened with tears, "I would be honored." I also reminded him that whenever that was, we would include whatever family was present. That said, he smiled and I left him to rest.

CHAPTER 22

TUESDAY, DECEMBER 21

When I Get Out of Here

When I arrived at Daddy's room today, his lunch tray was still on the bedside table, untouched. He was almost fully reclined and appeared rather uncomfortable. "How have you been?," I inquired. His response, "It's been terrible." He went on to tell me that he was in significant pain and had been for a good while. As I questioned him about his pain, he said it was a seven or eight, but had been so bad earlier that he wasn't sure if he had passed out or not. I was crushed. It is almost more than I can bear, seeing him fall from such a jovial mood just last evening to this: terrible pain that hinders even his ability to remain conscious. He informed me that he had not had any morphine since around midnight, but had pressed his call button three times. (He thought that was the right number, but wasn't sure since he was in such pain.) I told him that I would see what the accurate picture was, relative to the situation.

I went to the nurses' station and found the hall nurse. She said that he was due to have his morphine and had indeed not had any since midnight. I told her that he needed it and was in terrible pain. She said she would be "right there." (I wanted to say something to her about the lack of response, but realized that I needed to actually address it with a superior. For now, making sure he got relief was sufficient.) In a bit, she brought his morphine and asked him about his level of pain. He told her, "Five, maybe a six." After she gave him the morphine, I told him that we would eat after he had time for the pain to ease. I was going to find out the details of what had happened (or not happened, as the case might be) this morning. While he agreed for me to speak to the care plan coordinator, he was a bit apprehensive and told me that he was concerned about the potential negative element it could produce. Not being entirely sure what he meant, I asked him if he was afraid that the nurse in question might "get rough with you." He said that was his concern. I told him that the greater issue was his pain management and not whether the nurse got into trouble with her superior. I reminded him of what he had been through this morning and he agreed that I should follow through with my suggestion to speak to someone about it. He has not been treated inappropriately by anyone at the nursing home as far as I know; his care has been exemplary. We have been very satisfied with his stay.

I went to the care plan nurse and found her to be very understanding and apologetic. I also expressed to her that I knew Daddy was concerned to not "cause trouble," for fear of repercussions. I told her, however, that the situation this morning was unacceptable. She said that she would speak to the nurse ("That is my job") and for me to keep her up to speed if Daddy sensed any animosity from the nurse in question. I assured her that we had been very pleased with everything, but that this situation had to be resolved, to which she wholeheartedly agreed. He had told me that his pain this morning was "the worst since I was at the hospital in Lumberton."

I took time to speak with a couple of residents on the way back to his room. The care plan nurse got there ahead of me. When I entered the room, she was telling him that she thought the following would ensure that he did not suffer unnecessarily: instead of giving the morphine PRN (as needed) every two hours, make it scheduled for every two hours. I asked him if that was agreeable and he said that it was. We were reminded that he could always refuse it if he did not want to take it at the time it is offered. We both felt that was a reasonable "checks and balance" for his current situation. He told me later, "I am a dying man; what good is it for me to suffer with such intense pain?" I assured him that it was not beneficial; sharing that if his suffering was part of a process to get better, chemotherapy for instance, then the pain might be more acceptable. But in his case, that is not the way things are. He replied, "Exactly."

Eventually, he was clearly feeling less pain and had become more relaxed, so he tried to eat. He told me that he was having a headache in the left front section of his forehead. He also had a headache during the night, expressing that he couldn't understand, since he never has headaches. My mind immediately went back to what Scott had said the other night: cancer of this type can spread to the brain. That thought evidently had not crossed his mind, or if it did, he was not going to say anything about it, and neither was I. I pray to God that is *not* the case. He also said that he hurt in his right side just below his ribs, commenting after the rib statement that he wasn't sure what was going on "in there," but at this point it did not matter. I tried to reassure him.

He felt better as he tried to eat, so I opened his mail. He again had received several cards, mainly from people in Lumberton. I handed him them one at a time and he told me about the person who had written each one and how special this one or that one is. He continues to be positive about others and obviously has concern for them, in spite of his situation.

Sammy called and we both spoke to him. I filled him in on the morning's happenings, assuring him that we had "everything under control." He was all right with that, or so he said.

I informed Daddy that I had left a voice mail with the *Hospice* coordinator this morning, but had not heard anything back yet. He told me that he did not know what he would do without me. "I am privileged to help," I replied. He told me once more that I was his "advocate" (he has mentioned this several times), to which I responded, "That may be true, but mainly I am your son and simply want to try to help you any way that I can."

He ate about one-third of his dinner, said he was tired and asked me to let him back in his bed, which I did. I left him resting, if not comfortably, at least as close as was reasonably possible, considering the events of this morning.

* * *

Cindy and I came back just after 6:00 for an evening visit. I was apprehensive about how I might find him, but was pleasantly surprised. He was sitting up working on supper, having eaten almost all of it by then. He smiled and said, "Hey, Bud." I was relieved. My apprehension gave way to genuine happiness. We would have another time to talk when he would actually feel like he wanted to visit. Like Daddy, I do not look forward to the probability of the day when I come in and he is not able to communicate. I pray that we will have many more clear days before that happens.

He told me, as I questioned him, that he had taken two doses of morphine since I left this afternoon. He decided that it would be better to "head off the pain" instead of trying to "catch it up" by not taking the morphine when it is offered every two hours. I can tell that he is beginning to accept that increased pain medication and frequency are inevitable. He still wants to remain "as alert as I can for as long as I can." I hope that is for a long time to come.

Throughout the evening, Daddy did not talk as much as on previous nights. While he was not in pain, or at least significant pain, he was not as fully alert as he had been; it has to be the morphine. I did not sense that his thinking was clouded or that he was in a "fog," but simply very relaxed. I told him that he appeared to be relaxed, and he affirmed that he was comfortable.

I combed his hair as he finished his meal, telling him that he "looked better." He said he might have to go somewhere, such as the beach when "I get out of here." He smiled and said, "I'm kidding." I responded, "You never know."

He had several calls tonight: Carol, Harold, Mr. Lowry, Scott and J. W. and Sadie Lanier. J. W. and Sadie are Cindy's parents. They live in the Charity community of Duplin County near several of our other family members. Though retired, they do have two large chicken houses. They have been like a second set of parents to me, taking me in as a son from the first time we met back in 1983. David called as we visited as well.

When David called, Cindy and I began to prepare to leave. As Daddy talked to David I kissed him on the forehead and told him that I loved him. Once again, he affirmed every caller tonight and told each one how much their call means to him. I pray that his attitude continues to be so positive. I can certainly take a lesson from him on how to approach life with a positive attitude. In the last several weeks, I feel that I have been able to see the real man my father is and not the self-abusing façade that he has so often hidden behind through the years. I am thankful to God for such a wonderful experience and I will be grateful for as long as I live on this earth and also into eternity. Maybe Daddy and I can talk about God's goodness on that distant day in heaven. I look forward to many discussions with uncluttered heads and clear minds, being able to finally "know, even as (we) are also known."

CHAPTER 23

WEDNESDAY, DECEMBER 22

A Ton of Bricks

The care plan coordinator called me at home about 8:30 this morning. She told me that all was in place for *Hospice* to begin taking over Daddy's care tomorrow. There are a few items left to take care of, but they will be done today.

Not long after my conversation with her, Monica from *Hospice* called. She informed me that the nursing home had indeed gotten in touch with them, and all was in order. She asked if she and the *Hospice* social worker might meet with me today. I said, "About 4:30?" She said 4:00 was better. I agreed to meet them in Daddy's room at that time to discuss what the plan would be from this point on. Before we hung up, I told her that I would tell Daddy about the meeting when I see him later today.

After a moment, the realization of what we were discussing hit me like the proverbial "ton of bricks." While we sincerely want the services of *Hospice*, and while the services they so wonderfully provide are welcome, this is probably the beginning of the last phase of my father's life. I do not know if he has two weeks or two months, but know that we are now taking the "last step" in making sure, within our power, that he dies as "peacefully" as possible. *"God, give my father the grace to deal with it. Give us grace to be strong for him."*

* * *

Cindy and I arrived at Daddy's room around 12:00. He was resting, but opened his eyes and smiled as we entered. I asked him how he was doing. He said that he was comfortable; he appeared to be so to me as well. He told us that he had his morphine within the last 30 minutes or so and that he had "gotten along well" last night. I expressed how glad I was in not finding him as I did yesterday morning. He rolled his eyes and smiled. "Enough said," was his response.

They were holding his lunch until I got there. As soon as I arrived, the CNA soon came with it. He had barbeque boneless chicken, carrots, potato salad, water, tea, skim milk and two dough-nuts. (He asked me if they were *Krispy Kreme*, I told him "Sorry".) He smiled and said, "That's okay." As he was preparing to eat, I asked the CNA for scissors to trim his mustache, as it had grown over his upper-lip. As I trimmed, I also realized that he needed his teeth. When I finished with the scissors, I got his teeth for him. It took a little while before he said that he was ready to eat. Eventually, I opened his cards and gave him the "highlights." He had cards from seven or eight people, including one from David and Lynda, as well as a Sunday School class from a Baptist church in Lumberton. Every person in the class had evidently signed it. As I read the names, he cried openly.

He had begun to eat, but was really taking his time. It almost seems that he is not as hungry as he has been and he appears to have a more hollow look in his eyes as well. While Cindy and I were visiting with him, however, he managed to eat about three-fourths of his meal. I also brought coffee for the three of us. He drank a few swallows through a straw and ate one doughnut. Smiling, he commented, "I am as slow as an old man." During the time of eating, he had trouble with gas in his throat (he has reflux) and said it was hard to get the food down. Overall, it wasn't bad, however, and he ate without too much trouble. He told me that he had a story for me today. He perked up as he told it, though his strength to talk seems less than on previous visits.

The story has to do with Fred Hedrick, a blind judge from North Carolina. As part of receiving aid to attend Carolina, Daddy agreed to help a blind student on campus. There were three or four on campus at that time. Part of the responsibilities included rooming with the person. His schedule had to at least compliment Fred's schedule, so they took some classes together. But mainly he had to "Be where you could carry (sic) him to class or he could wait outside your door." Daddy said that Fred was "not typical judge material, but extremely smart." He became blind at the age of 12 when he was hit in the face with a rock. He began attending "blind school" at that time and stayed with it until he went to UNC. He had studied some on Broadway, being an "operatic tenor." However, his blindness did not allow him to continue that pursuit, and he came to UNC to study art and simply get a liberal arts education.

He did well in college and had, as Daddy put it, "a photographic memory without the photographs." He would have Daddy read certain portions of books, writers such as "Tom Paine" for instance. He would literally remember the material and was able to get to the "bottom line." That is why he ultimately made such a good judge, Daddy said.

As told to me by him, Daddy arrived in Chapel Hill on a cold, rainy, October day, somewhere near his birthday. He was trying to find his dorm, "the cheapest one on campus," when he came across some upperclassmen. They told him he needed to take the bus back to another place; that was where his dorm was located. He walked one-half mile to get back on the bus in the rain, only to discover that he had been right next to his dorm all along. He told me this about the guy who had led him astray, and I quote: "I would remember his face, but his name would go down in infamy," he chuckled.

Daddy's dorm situation was not the best, since there were four guys in a small room (including him and Fred), with only one bathroom. The room had two bunk beds. Daddy only had what he could carry when he arrived. The rest of his belongings arrived two days later in a steamer trunk given to him by Frank Holden, Aunt Ruby's husband, from Richmond, Virginia.

Daddy and Fred fast became "good friends." He was his "reader and roommate, and that made for a good situation." He would tell Daddy that he wanted a certain thing read and Daddy would tell him, "Bring me the book and I'll do it." Later in life, he became a good judge, able to cut through the red tape. In their second year together, they ended up in a different dorm, but stayed on the first floor because Fred was unable to negotiate steps very well. This was before the days when the disabled were considered in the construction of buildings.

Fred would often sing in the bathroom until the walls would literally shake. I asked Daddy what type of songs he would sing and he quoted the following words written by Rudyard Kipling:

> *On the road to Mandalay*
> *Where the flyin'-fishes play*
> *An' the dawn comes up like thunder outer*
> *China 'crost the Bay!*

He also shared a joke that Fred told about Betty Grable that I must admit was funny. We both laughed.

We talked about *Hospice* coming in as I prepared to leave. I could tell that, while he certainly sees the need of them getting on board, Daddy seemed to have a slight hesitation as we discussed it. He told me, after some prodding, that he knew the connotation of what goes with *Hospice* getting involved. I reminded him that they have resources for the entire family and not just him alone. It is better to get them involved and all of us acclimated early, rather than later. He cried openly. He is concerned about how it will make the family feel, especially Carol. He accepts, nevertheless, that it is undoubtedly for the best. It was a rather somber discussion, but we have clearly reached another stage in the dying process, though he hopefully has many more days left yet.

I asked him what made him cry, and his answer, to me at least, was profound. It obviously is a reference to spiritual enlightenment. He said, "Only my eye that cannot see cries, the eye that can see does not." (He is blind in his left eye and has been for a few years now.) I could tell by his expression that he was implying that his eye that "could not see" was a reference to the dying process and all of the unknown things that are "not seen." Those things bring sadness, uncertainty and tears. But the reference to the eye that "can see," which does *not* cry, refers to the eventual outcome that can be seen: heaven and peace. He was referring perhaps, to that time when God "will wipe every tear from their eyes. There will be no more death or mourning or crying or pain, for the old order of things has passed away" (Revelation 21:4). It will be a time when we will have no more suffering or pain. I hugged him, trying to encourage him, and left.

* * *

At 4:00 we had our meeting with *Hospice* in Daddy's room. We met with the social worker, a nurse and a social worker trainee. The social worker introduced everyone to us and took a chair beside Daddy's bed, next to the window. She had several forms to go over and needed some information on his immediate history, along with the names and residences of all of his children. She began by asking him about his oldest, and progressed down the line from there. He started with Sammy and then elaborated on each one of us, including the grandchildren and our various occupations. While she probably didn't need all of the information that he was providing, she was very gracious in allowing him time to share the additional history on each of us. Several times, tears came to his eyes and he wiped them with his thumb and forefinger, as he often does when he cries. I was moved myself and the tears flowed freely. It was very touching to hear him tell how proud he is of each and every one of his children, without exception.

After she finished with the family information, she had four forms for Daddy to sign, each on a clipboard. I helped steady the clipboard as he began the process. Before the first was signed, he said he might need to read it because he could be "signing a marriage license." The others and I laughed at his humor.

After she finished, she turned it over to the *Hospice* nurse who asked him some general medical questions. (He deferred to me to give a rundown of the last several weeks and how he came to be at the nursing home.) She had him turn on his right side. He pulled himself on the bed railing without a tremendous amount of difficulty. She examined his bedsores and checked his breathing. After a short time, she had him turn once again over onto his back. His blood pressure was 136/60 while his temperature was 97.9.

The social worker asked if he would like to have a *Hospice* volunteer come by to visit. They are trained to make calls, and sometimes it is good to have someone besides the family to come by, she explained. Daddy told her that would be fine. She also mentioned that while he had a chaplain in "your son," the *Hospice* chaplain would come by if he liked. She mentioned her name. I told her that I know Jeannette; she is a good friend of mine and actually helps me with the nursing home service regularly. She commented on her sense of humor. I told Daddy that she would be very encouraging. He said to have her come, commenting, "I'll take all that I can get." She also shared the phone information with us, relative to the nurse on call and other pertinent items. As they stood to leave, I saw Sammy coming up to the window. I told them that the "good old boy," as Daddy had described him earlier, was here. They laughed when he came up and knocked on the window.

Sammy, Sandra, Vada and Austin soon came into the room. I introduced the *Hospice* team to them. The social worker stated that she would be back and that Daddy was a joy to visit, "I can tell."

I stayed for a bit with Sammy and his family. Before I left, however, I asked them to help get Daddy's supper for him as it had arrived by now. I also asked them to take care of his teeth, to give me a call before they left (they would be spending the night with us) and that I would order pizza for us to pick up and eat for supper at the house. I hugged Daddy goodbye, told him I loved him, and left him in their care.

* * *

As I think about what Daddy said this afternoon before we met with Hospice, and as I think about his weeping, especially at the beginning of our meeting with them, I feel that he and I have crossed a psychological, and perhaps spiritual, barrier. The meeting itself, the turning over of his care to Hospice, was a hurdle that we wanted to put off facing for as long as possible. The "beginning of the end," as some refer to it, has indeed started with this initial meeting. But the larger implications are more significant: not only have we crossed that barrier, but also we are now committed to that race. While I know that Hospice provides more than simple comfort and support to a dying man, I also share Daddy's thoughts expressed earlier, that this is the last phase of his life. We are now in totally uncharted waters.

"But the best of all is, God is with us."

CHAPTER 24

THURSDAY, DECEMBER 23

The Beginning of Letting Go

S ammy, Sandra, Vada, Austin, Cindy and I arrived at the nursing home around 11:30. Daddy was almost prostrate in the bed. His lunch came almost as soon as we arrived. There were not enough chairs, so I went to find one or two more.

They had been waiting for me to arrive before actually bringing his lunch. He had meatloaf and other trimmings. I commented that he really likes meatloaf and spaghetti to the rest of the family there.

Since he wasn't ready to eat yet, we elevated him a little so that he could see us better. From the moment he began to speak, I could tell a change in him, a couple of things actually:

He was not as bright as usual, not smiling or even talking much. He almost seemed depressed.

His statements came with more difficulty than usual, i. e., he could not seem to carry out a meaningful conversation. He would forget words, or not be able to finish a thought.

I don't know if his morphine is making him foggy, or if he has crossed another threshold in the dying process. I asked him about his pain medications and he wasn't sure what he had taken today. To me, it was another issue that shows the difficulty he is having today. He has not had issues of memory or thought since he has been here and, at this time, I am not sure what the problem really is. Nevertheless, we began to visit.

Sammy had brought quite a few pictures that included his family and our extended family's times at White Lake, pictures of the flood of 1999 (Sammy and Sandra lost their house) and other events. Daddy perked up some as Sammy stood by his bed and showed him various pictures and talked briefly about them. Daddy acted interested, but seemed a bit distant.

During this time, his lunch was untouched. I finally encouraged them that he probably needed to eat something. We warmed his plate and got things ready. He ate a bite or two of his food, but like the picture viewing time, did not seem very interested in eating. While he would not admit that he was in much pain, it seemed to me that the pain and/or issues discussed earlier were keeping him from having much interest in anything today. For the next two hours he nibbled, but never did eat much.

As we talked, I noticed something unusual. (Sammy said that he noticed it as well later.) When a couple of points relative to the drug store were mentioned, he turned his head toward me and asked me about it. It was more than him simply looking for me to help him get some information across, which he has done in the past weeks. He was seeing me as David, who obviously knows all about issues with the store. He did this twice. I simply responded, "I do not know." Again, is this the morphine, or is this his illness progressing more, or even something else? I am not sure.

As he talked more, he had difficulty in getting his points across. He said, "I'm getting as slow as Frank was," referring to our uncle who died with cancer this past January; he was Daddy's brother. Daddy's mood continued to be subdued. He stated, after my prodding, that he was in more pain and that his head hurt. He could "not understand that," he commented, with a frown. I asked him if he wanted me to call for his morphine; he said to do so. I walked to the nurses' station to tell her. She soon came with his Percocet and morphine, but as she left the room, I asked her about his inability to focus. She told me that it could be related to the morphine, or even to his pain. She also said that he had indeed been in tremendous pain this morning. His pain now occurs in his head, his back and his right side. She assured me that she would do all she could to make sure that he was not in pain. I thanked her as she turned to leave. I feel very good about his nursing situation at this time. His morphine could be given every hour, one-half of a dose. That would help control his pain better. I do not know if Daddy is willing, however, to do that yet.

With his medication given and no progress on his lunch, I asked him if we might have communion together. He said that he would like to, so I retrieved the communion set from his bedside table and filled seven cups with juice. I chose to read the birth narrative of Christ from Luke, chapter 2 and the Passover meal of Christ from the gospel of Mark, chapter 14. I talked about that Jesus' birth was ultimately about his death for us, dying for our salvation and suffering. I prayed the prayer of consecration and served the bread; we all ate together. I then served the juice and we all drank together. I had another prayer, laying my hand on Daddy's left shoulder. I prayed for his peace and health and also for all of us. After we were through praying, I read a passage from Corinthians:

> [16]*That is why we never give up. Though our bodies are dying, our spirits are being renewed every day.* [17]*For our present troubles are quite small and won't last very long. Yet they produce for us an immeasurably great glory that will last forever!* [18]*So we don't look at the troubles we can see right now; rather, we look forward to what we have not yet seen. For the troubles we see will soon be over, but the joys to come will last forever (2 Corinthians 4:16-18, NLT).*

All present had moist eyes as we drew things to a close.

As Sammy and his family prepared to leave, they presented Daddy with a replica model of the "Firestone" plane. They also gave him a portable CD player/radio that he could listen to in bed. It included several music CDs, as well as a set of *Prairie Home Companion* installments. Daddy listened a few seconds, but was obviously tired. The CNAs came in to turn and change him. Telling him goodbye, we all left the room. It was well after 3:00, and he has had a rather busy afternoon.

Some observations:

His headaches are increasing in frequency (intensity?).

He still holds off on the morphine and increasing his other pain medications. I am sure that his earlier statement is still true, "I want to remain as alert as I can for as long as I can." He is still not being totally truthful about his pain level. He may mention that he is having some pain, but rarely tells me when he has had a very bad time of pain.

He appears to me, at least, to be more subdued and perhaps depressed, though he will not admit it. He may be concerned that an admission would prompt more medication. He continues to deny that he needs anything for anxiety.

* * *

I returned to visit him around 6:00, alone. He was sitting up eating his supper. I joked with him about eating "breakfast for supper," since he was eating scrambled eggs, sausage, cooked prunes, tea, water and milk. He had eaten almost all of the eggs and had one of two sausages left. He would eventually eat everything but some of the prunes. I'm sure that he was hungry after not eating any significant lunch.

His difficulty with focusing his thoughts continues this afternoon. I do not see any difference from this morning. As he finished his supper, I read him a few of the cards that he had received this afternoon. He had three from people in Lumberton. I read them while he, of course, graciously commented on each person, albeit with some difficulty. He continues to have that drive and desire to encourage and lift up others. He also had one from his sister, Sissie. As I read it, he began to sob. I cried as well, but was able to finish it. I commented on how much he is loved. All he could say was, "I am blessed." I responded, "We all are."

As we were finishing with her card, the phone rang. After several rings I told him that based on the time, "That must be David." He nodded as he continued to wipe his eyes and I answered the phone. David said, after my greeting, that I sounded tired. I told him that I was fine. He inquired as to why it took me so long to answer the phone, so I told him that we were busy finishing up reading some of Daddy's cards; that seemed to satisfy him. I was reluctant to tell him that we both had been having a "crying spell."

David talked with Daddy after I gave Daddy time to compose himself. After several minutes, Daddy gave the phone back to me. I walked out into the hall and talked with David briefly, informing him about Daddy's inability to stay focused. He had noticed it and said, "We may be at the point where we will have good days and bad days." I agreed with him. We soon brought our conversation to a close; it was rather somber.

Daddy looked relaxed when I came back into the room, so I asked him if he wanted me to call for his pain medications. He said to do so. I walked to the nurses' station and requested his morphine. I also asked about the side effects of it. She said that it slowed respiration and brought relaxation to the patient. She said that initially, it can cause some loss of focus, but that is generally short-lived. I shared my concern about his sedation and the change I had noted. She was very compassionate and allowed me to talk freely about my observations. She also told me that he had one half-dose of morphine at about 5:30, and that she felt it was "your sister" who had called earlier this morning. Daddy had been unable to talk with Carol; he was in so much pain. As usual, he had not mentioned the call, or the pain, to me.

She brought him the full dose of morphine and his Percocet, telling him about taking one-half dose every hour instead of the full dose every two hours. He doesn't need to "get behind" on the pain. She said that she would give him a full dose at 9:00 and 11:00, with the Percocet at 11:00 as well, before she goes off of her shift. He seemed to agree with her recommendations. He then took the Percocet and she exited his room. I helped him hold the morphine so that he would not spill any of it. He drank it all and laid his head back on the pillow. He had told the nurse, before she left, that if he could get settled he normally can sleep several hours without much trouble.

As he was swallowing his morphine, Sandra, from the drug store, called. I told her that he was in pain and literally had just taken his pain medications. She said that she felt perfectly comfortable talking with me, so I filled her in as well as I could. She told me that she was sending Daddy a Christmas package by David when he comes this Sunday and she asked me to tell Daddy that she loved him and that he was in her thoughts. She also asked me to say a prayer for him on her behalf. (I later told Daddy what she had said and we had prayer together.)

She had asked me how I was doing. I was honest with her and said that I was exhausted. She encouraged me to try and enjoy Christmas, even though it will be hard to do, she admitted. I told her we would do our best and thanked her on behalf of Daddy for her call.

Before leaving, I dimmed Daddy's lights and turned the TV on low volume to the *History Channel*. He said he wanted to hear it as he went to sleep. As I prepared to leave, he tried to tell me that dying was really the only thing left to do. He said that he felt "near death," but knows that "God is with us." On that, I left him to rest.

* * *

As I reflect on today, my heart is closer to letting go of him. Obviously, I do not know how long it will be, but certainly feel that we have crossed new territory today. It he agrees to take enough medications to control his pain, I sense that the "times of stories" are becoming a thing of the past. I now realize that just as he wants to remain alert, I want him to remain alert for me...and all of us. However, I also acknowledge that we are simply delaying the inevitable.

"God, help him to let go and help us to let go as well. May all of us, and Daddy most of all, have Your grace during this time, a grace that truly is sufficient for our need."

CHAPTER 25

FRIDAY, DECEMBER 24

More Than Clouds

I arrived at the nursing home today, alone, just after noon. Daddy was in bed and in a rather dazed way. It took me about 30 seconds to ascertain that he was even worse than I had left him last night. He was trying to position himself with his arms by pulling on the bed rails. He was almost constantly moaning and saying things like, "It hurts," or "Oh God," or "Help me, Jesus."

I questioned him about his pain, and he could only moan and look at me as if he didn't see me. Occasionally, he did say, "I'm all right," but it was obvious that he was not. He appeared to be in great pain, so I went to ask about his morphine. He had received his last dose five hours earlier, around 7:00 a. m. She soon brought it and he drank the full amount without any questions. I began to feed him. Before I did, however, I called the *Hospice* number and got in touch with Patti. I told her my observations:

He is disoriented and cannot focus.
He appears to be in significant pain.
I can see major changes from yesterday, but actually began noticing that he was different on Wednesday evening.

She told me that if it was all right, she would come after she saw one other patient. I told her I would try to feed him his lunch since he really was not able to feed himself.

I went back in and found him still behaving as if he was very uncomfortable, unable to sit still, moaning and crying. He cried very hard, at least once, and was tearful quite a bit.

He had a hotdog, bowl of slaw, French fries and a brownie. I managed to get him to eat the meat from the hotdog and a taste of everything else. He eventually told me that he was done and refused to eat any more. I did, however, get him to eat a piece of candy with me.

As we looked out of the window, I asked him if he knew what waited up there, beyond the clouds? He nodded "No" and said, "What?" I said, "Heaven. There's more than clouds floating around." He cried some more. I would take the tissue and dab his eyes each time that he cried. I felt so sorry for him and actually cried a bit myself.

I changed the subject and told him that the *Hospice* nurse was coming today. I wanted to see about increasing his pain medications if he would consent to do so. I asked him if we might do that and he said, "Yes." I also mentioned that Carol was coming. He looked at me quizzically and asked, "Carol?" I said, "Carol Ann, do you know who she is?" He responded, "Yes, my daughter," and began to cry more. I wiped his eyes and stepped out to get a cup of coffee from the break room area. I was unsure how to proceed.

As I neared the room again, I saw that one of the CNAs, Patricia, was at his side and singing to him. She was soothingly singing *He Touched Me* as she wiped his face with a napkin. His eyes were closed and he seemed peaceful. I came into the room as she finished and thanked her. I told him, "You can't get music like that just anywhere, Daddy, and it's free." He gave me his "hmm" look and smiled. The song was a real blessing to him...and me. I was praying that God would indeed touch my father once again as she sang.

I read him some sections from a book that Sammy had brought, then asked him if he remembered when he quoted the first two lines of *Blessed Assurance* in the hospital, and I finished saying the lines to it. He shook his head, "No." I sang the first and last verses and then said, "Well, I'm not the best singer in the world, but at least I sing better than Sammy," jokingly. He did not respond.

Around 2:00 Patti, the *Hospice* nurse, arrived. She asked Daddy some questions and checked his vitals. She also had him hold her fingers to see how strong his grip was. His grip was good, his blood pressure was 100/60 and his temperature was 98.7. She also checked his breathing and did not detect any congestion. When done, she told him that she needed to speak to "your son for a minute. Is that O.K?" He said that it was. We went into the TV area and sat near the door that opens onto the patio for the 100 hall. On the way, she commented what a sweet man that Daddy is. After we sat down, she informed me that his cancer was still in check, but that he was having an "Alzheimer's episode." She had seen it many times, commenting that her mother had Alzheimer's as well. Asking her if he would come out of it, she said, "He might, but there is no way to know for sure." I revealed his history of alcoholism to her. She said that alcoholics tend to require higher doses of pain medication(s) than those who are not alcoholics. She reiterated that he should take the morphine as prescribed, every two hours, and that we would see about moving his patch from 25 mcg. to 50 mcg. on Monday. I told her that I certainly understood what she was saying, and that we would do all we can for him. She said that watching TV was good for his condition as well, as it stimulates brain activity.

I told her that we, as a family, were hoping that he would not have to suffer for an extended period of time. "I do not believe that he will linger very long," she responded soberly. I thanked her as she left. Returning to his room, I told Daddy that I loved him and would see him later for supper. He nodded, but did not say anything.

* * *

It is amazing how God has allowed Daddy to be alert for several weeks, to get his business, family and spiritual life in order; he is ready for heaven. That is a tremendous thought, especially as I think about the possibility that I may never clearly communicate with him again. God has truly given him, and us, a wonderful gift!

Alzheimer's is a terrible disease. Cancer is a terrible disease. But do they actually complement one another? Alzheimer's prevents a person from being truly aware of their cancer and cancer prevents a person with Alzheimer's from suffering for so long. Is this actually another blessing from God? Even if Daddy "comes to" mentally, it will just be a matter of time before he goes out again. His request "to stay as alert as I can for as long as I can" may have been fulfilled. How ironic, though, that it may be Alzheimer's that ultimately takes away his alertness and not morphine or some other drug. God knows best. If this is the way it is to end, I am going to try and look at it from a positive perspective if I can.

* * *

I called Carol to let her know about Daddy, since I was aware that she was coming today. She took the news well and reminded me that Daddy behaved the same way for a time in Lumberton when he was in the hospital, only to come out of it. (I have had no knowledge of that episode.) He later referred to it as if he was "watching a movie." He may come around again; we will have to wait and see. Carol will call Scott and Sammy while we agreed that I would tell David about these developments when he calls tonight.

* * *

Cindy and I went to be with Daddy for supper. Carol and Mike were already there; she was helping him eat. His condition was about the same, though she did manage to get him to eat at least most of his supper. He still spoke in short sentences and seemed at a loss as to where he was. Eventually, he had enough supper and told Carol that he was done.

The rest of our time together was spent talking to him and drying his eyes when he cried. He did say, "Where am I?" at least a couple of times and it seemed obvious to me that he is trying hard to figure out what is happening. He cannot quite "get it together," but he appears to be trying. He cried several times but didn't seem to be in pain, just frustrated and at a loss to totally express himself. He would still smile, on occasion, and it is easy to see that he is trying hard to come out of it; the wheels are turning. One thing about my father: he will not give up on anything. As long as there is a chance that he can come back, he will fight. I can see that tonight; but he may be running out of chances. I honestly do not know.

Mr. Lowry called and I shared the news on Daddy. He seemed both genuinely bothered and saddened. David also called, speaking of the similarities between this "episode" and the one in Lumberton at the hospital a few weeks ago, just as Carol had shared. He holds out hope that Daddy will come to himself again, just as he did then.

Cindy and I got ready to leave. I kissed Daddy and hugged him goodbye. He got very emotional. It breaks my heart to think that this man, my father, who was laughing and sharing so many stories about his life and the life of our family just 48 hours ago, has now been reduced to this. May God help us all. We are really going to need that grace that we have spoken about so much recently. I thank God that Daddy made his peace while he still could.

I told Carol that I would see them in the morning when we bring Daddy's Christmas present to him. She and Mike have made arrangements to stay in a local hotel while we will be going out of town to be with the rest of the family for the holiday. Cindy and I soon left, but with very heavy hearts indeed.

CHAPTER 26

SATURDAY, DECEMBER 25

A Faraway Look

On the way to see Daddy this morning, Carol called. She and Mike were already at the nursing home. I asked her how Daddy was and she said, "No better." They had brought his breakfast before they arrived and Daddy had tried to drink his coffee without assistance. He ended up spilling it on himself. Carol was composed, but clearly distraught. They were cleaning him up at that point. I told her that we would be there in five or six minutes. I asked her if he had gotten burned, and she said that he had not; the coffee was not that hot.

Upon arriving, we found Mike and Carol outside, near Daddy's window. He was putting up a bird feeder on a pole in the mulched area near Daddy's room. After finishing, he put up a small, window-mounted feeder on Daddy's window as well. I'm sure that Daddy will enjoy the feeders; he loves to look out of the window.

The four of us went back inside together, waiting just outside of his room. In a few minutes, they were finished with Daddy and we went in to see him. He was slightly elevated in the bed and had a pillow under his left side, so that he was facing the window and the new bird feeders. He appeared fairly tranquil, but still had that "spacey, faraway look" in his eyes. The TV had not been changed from the *History Channel*. While he will look at the screen for a few moments at the time, I don't believe he can enjoy the programs, yet the *Hospice* nurse did tell me that the TV was good stimulation for someone in his condition. While he was not "himself," he seemed to be slightly more alert than he was last night. And while he did not call our names, he smiled more, even though he cried several times while we were there. He complained of pain also.

We were able to get a pillow to place under his right arm. That seemed to make him more comfortable, but he still complained of pain. We raised his blind so he could see the bird feeders. That seemed to please him, but eventually we had to put the blinds down and turn off the light in his room. He kept complaining of a headache and said "I didn't know it would be like this." Could he be talking about his headache (which seemed severe), or perhaps his struggle to keep his thoughts together, or even his overall condition? There is no way to know and I'm sure he would not have been able to explain what he meant at that point anyway.

Previously, we had asked for the morphine. They brought it and he took it all. We asked the nurse about getting the morphine scheduled every two hours, instead of "as needed." We also discussed increasing the patch from 25 to 50 mcg. She would call *Hospice* and see if these two items would be taken care of today, she promised.

While we waited for the morphine to kick in (he had not had any since 12:00 last night), Cindy and I gave him his Christmas card. (I had to open it and read it to him and also helped him open his present.) We had pictures made for our church's pictorial directory and gave Daddy a five by seven in a nice wooden frame. His only comment was, "Looks like a preacher to me." We all laughed at his humor. He directed us to move a plant toward the back and put the picture on the top of the cabinet that holds his clothes. It is also covered with cards because as he receives them, we tape them to the front and the side of the cabinet. We moved the plant and put the picture where he directed. I had also brought an extension cord, so we were finally able to light the Christmas tree that David and Lynda brought on that first visit so many weeks ago. We also lit the "Sam's Pharmacy" given to Daddy by Marlena, whose mother resides across the hall. In the process, we had to unplug the digital clock. *At this point, I do not desire to be reminded of days or hours anyway.*

While it may sound like he was rather cognizant, he was actually still struggling significantly. He kept trying to tell us certain things but was unable to complete most of his thoughts. He also was very uncomfortable and kept saying, over and over, "Oh boy," as if he was flabbergasted that he could not get his words or thoughts together.

In a while, the morphine began to take effect and he gradually settled down, so we decided to go. Carol and Mike walked out with us. Cindy and I were heading home for Christmas but wanted to be back in time to visit Daddy tomorrow after lunch. I told Carol and Mike that we would see them at Sammy's tonight. We are going to meet there, as we always do at Christmas, though it will feel much different than previous years.

Upon reflection, while Daddy is suffering, I am actually gaining tremendous experience in dealing with those I have so often ministered to over the years. I now know what it is like to have a loved one suffer with cancer. I now know what it is like to have a loved one suffer with Alzheimer's disease. I now know what it is like to have a close family member as a resident in a nursing facility. I now know what it is like having a loved one for an extended stay in the hospital. I want to care for Daddy, but I also want to see the other facets of this situation. I want to understand what God is teaching us as a family and not simply what is happening to Daddy. While pain management is the primary concern, there are always lessons to be learned if we are open to accept them. I certainly have new empathy for those who deal with the various struggles we are facing.

Also, what kind of life can my father expect if he indeed comes to himself again? He has cancer, he has Alzheimer's, he is paralyzed, he has no control over his bodily functions, he has bedsores and is gradually losing his grip on all that is familiar. I know from our earlier conversations that this single thing is what Daddy was most afraid of: not being alert and being unable to communicate. He wanted to "remain as alert as I can, for as long as I can."

"Please God, may his suffering be short."

* * *

Carol called Scott from Sammy's tonight; he is with Daddy in High Point. Scott spoke with me also. Daddy has been having trouble swallowing (cancer related?). He managed to feed himself unassisted, however, for supper. Scott said that Daddy had eaten 90% of his supper, which is good. Carol said that he ate virtually none of his lunch. I have noticed over the last several weeks, that this has been the case many days: little lunch, good eating at supper.

Scott also said that they had added another 25 mcg. patch for a total of 50. Daddy is still in "left field." Scott told me that he was "catching butterflies," a reference to exaggerated, seemingly meaningless hand gestures (meaningless to us, at least). These gestures could be related to Alzheimer's, or they may be the beginning of his journey from this consciousness to the next. As with so many other things with Daddy now, we will probably not know what these things mean or symbolize. We can only conjecture and *try* to make sense out of them.

CHAPTER 27

SUNDAY, DECEMBER 26

Breaking the Spell

We all met at Sammy's house last night. Those present were: Mama and Ronald, David and Lynda, Carol and Mike, Jason, Eric and Kelly, Lois Henderson (Mike's mother), Sammy and Sandra, Vada, Austin, Cindy and myself. The occasion was somber, but jovial at times as well. Various family members came together at different times throughout the evening and discussed everything from Daddy's condition to potential funeral arrangements. Delwood, Beverly and Kylee also came by a little later. Cindy and I left around 9:00 and spent the night with her parents, J. W. and Sadie Lanier.

Today, we received a call at 8:30, informing us that services had been cancelled at *Bethel Wesleyan*, our home church in the Rose Hill area. Carol and Mike left very early to go back to High Point. We have had sleet and freezing rain overnight, so Cindy and I ended up staying with her parents tonight. We will not get back to High Point until tomorrow. Carol, Mike, Ashly, Sammy (Ashly's husband) and Scott are staying at our house overnight. I have talked with both Scott and Carol today. Daddy has had three doses of morphine and is resting comfortably, although he has not eaten very much breakfast or lunch. They are at our house in Thomasville, planning to freshen up and go back to see Daddy after they eat supper. Daddy is comfortable at this time.

Scott and Carol have both seen Daddy's bedsores and they are very serious. We realized that they were bad when he arrived at the nursing home in High Point on November 16th. It is critical that he continue to be moved every two hours since he is not in as much pain when he is off them. As they are there in High Point looking after him, Cindy and I are in Rose Hill, stuck in the bad weather. With some down time on my hands, I have been thinking.

Today is the first day since November 16th that I have not seen Daddy at least once. Most days, though not all, I have been by twice. I only went by in the morning on both Thanksgiving and Christmas. I am having a somewhat difficult time not being with him after 40 consecutive days. But in all honesty, I feel a sense of relief in knowing that I cannot get to the nursing home today even though I would want to if possible. I fully trust all of my other siblings and know that they can care for him as good as, and in some respects better than I. Still, it is an adjustment. I have crossed a hurdle, not dissimilar to the ones that Daddy is crossing one by one. Just as he is letting go, little by little, being away from him after almost six consecutive weeks reminds me, rather abruptly I might add, that I surely must let go, little by little, of him. This separation has "broken the spell" of *ultimate* responsibility that I feel for him. I must do what I can, but also allow Sammy, David, Carol and Scott to do what they can as well. It is their responsibility and their desire to do so.

"Lord, give me the freedom to leave Daddy in their hands now, and most of all, in Yours. Protect them as they help and as they travel. Draw our family together and help us all to do what we must do. Also help us to let go, 'little by little.'"

CHAPTER 28

MONDAY, DECEMBER 27

I Could Stay Here All Night

Cindy and I left her parents to travel back to High Point after breakfast today. We passed through some areas of snow, especially around Benson, and saw ice on the trees for much of the way until that point. From Sanford on, the snow gradually disappeared. Benson was said to have four inches of snow on the ground.

As we were on the road, Carol called me. Daddy was experiencing significant pain and had made both her and Scott promise to not make him take the morphine. He will take it at times, however, when Carol is not in the room. Is he afraid of the impact that it might have on her? Is he protecting her? I told her to contact *Hospice* to see if we might get help with his patch; perhaps it is time to increase it. That particular route seems to be the one of least resistance. She said that they would get in touch with the *Hospice* nurse today.

Daddy has times when he is more alert than others. His mental state is improving some, but he still asks them where he is. Why is he there? Carol told him that he had broken his leg and also that he had developed pneumonia. (Both are true.) She told me that she did not want to remind him of the cancer. She asked me if I thought that was the right thing to do. I told her that it was. She told him that he was having these questions because of an Alzheimer's episode. I'm not sure what his response was to that bit of information.

Carol, Mike, Ashly, Sammy (her husband) and Scott said that they would all stay until Cindy and I arrived. Daddy has not eaten any breakfast. That means that he has missed four meals in a row, having eaten nothing yesterday either.

* * *

We arrived at his room shortly after lunch. Everyone was still there, plus an anesthesiologist friend from Lumberton. He came late yesterday and spent the night in High Point. He has been in rehab for drug and alcohol addiction for a while. Daddy was clutching a blue, one-year "AA" chip that the doctor had given him. Daddy was still tearful, but seemed significantly more alert, especially as compared to the past few days. He smiled and became tearful when I bent down to kiss him. He was still in pain and did not eat any lunch.

Scott had spoken with *Hospice* about a couple of things:

We need to secure a mattress that automatically inflates and deflates to keep pressure off of the bedsores. It is very similar to what he had while in the hospital here in High Point.

It is time to begin to explore beginning a new type of therapy for Daddy's bedsores.

As we talked, the new mattress arrived. They used the lift to put Daddy in a gerry chair. Surprisingly, it was not rough on him at all. While they got his mattress ready we pushed him into the TV room so he could see outside near the patio on his hall. He immediately brightened, drinking some Ensure and coffee. We asked them to bring him some soft food. While we waited, I pushed him down his hall and then down the 200 hall. We passed Scott B., who is paralyzed and has MS, a resident of the facility for 17 years. I introduced him and Daddy. Scott B. commented that his first name was Samuel as well. Daddy waved goodbye and we rode back to the TV room on his hall. His food soon came; he ate three-fourths of a pimento cheese sandwich on a hamburger roll. He said that his appetite was "terrific." That, and the milk that came with it, was all he ate. All but Scott, Cindy and me had left by then.

An announcement came over the PA system that a pianist and flutist would be giving a concert at 4:00 in the dining hall on the first floor near Daddy's room. When I asked Daddy about attending, he said he definitely would like to go, so we began pushing him again. Arriving at the dining hall, we found six other residents waiting. We positioned Daddy where he could see the piano, while I sat on one side and Scott on the other. After several minutes, when the musicians did not show up, Cindy asked if she should play. I told her that would be great. She played several Christmas hymns, plus *At Calvary*, requested by Scott B., the resident who was there as well. Daddy loved the music, stating, "I could stay here all night and listen to this." I remarked, "Cindy would probably eventually run out of material." He continued smiling and looked very peaceful and restful. It was a very positive experience for him. I told him that I would see about getting him up as much as we can now that we realize that the lift does not cause him any pain. I also told him that perhaps we could get him to the worship services on the second floor. (They are held each Sunday and Wednesday mornings in that dining hall.) He actually has attended a couple of them during his time here. I feel like he liked that idea.

* * *

At 6:00, they put him back to bed without incident. He soon was dozing and very comfortable. It seems clear that the mattress is a very good idea. I have seen him relaxed about as much as I can remember in recent days. He took morphine before they put him back in bed and again at 7:00. He would take another dose at 9:00.

Scott and I talked with him for a good while, one of us on either side of his bed. We talked about a lot of things since his mind seemed to be working at 90% or so. He was still very relaxed and commented that he was quite satisfied and settled. I reminded him that his life, and all of our lives, would go on after this one. He is afraid of the process of dying and letting go. He continued, nevertheless, to remain alert, but restful.

He spoke to several people who called on the phone: David, Mr. Lowry and Sandra, from the store. At one point, while Scott and I talked between ourselves out in the hall, the phone rang. Cindy answered it. It was a person from Lumberton, a customer. She said that Daddy had helped her family last winter and that they would not have made it without his help. I asked him about her later and he said one of his cards was from her. As I think back, I remember seeing her name on one of the cards.

While Scott and I were in the hall, Cindy said that Daddy had fallen asleep. He said, "We need to go to Graham's store" and smiled a very big smile. Graham's store was the local store in the Northeast community where Daddy was born and raised. I remember Granddaddy Roland taking me there as a very young child and getting a bag full of "penny candy," including bubblegum cigars, candy cigarettes and a "Brownie" chocolate drink. Cindy sensed that Daddy was dreaming about family already deceased, perhaps Uncle Frank; we will never know. I pray that all of his dreams will be pleasant ones.

As Cindy and I prepared to leave at 9:00, Daddy commented to Scott and me, "I am so glad that you both are here with me." *Daddy, we are too.*

* * *

Scott called me at home at 10:30, asking if he could stay the night with us and drive back to Tennessee in the morning. We said certainly he could do that; we are open to anyone staying with us who needs to come and spend some time with Daddy. He did not get to the house, however, until close to 12:00. We stayed up and talked for 30 minutes or so before going to bed. After 10:30, Daddy had told Scott that he had some questions. Scott told me that they talked about the following:

They settled issues between them (if there were any).
They discussed Daddy's history with Barbara, Scott's mother.
Scott told him what he might expect during the dying process.

Scott said that they discussed each one in detail as well as other things. He also said that he was very encouraged and feels as if Daddy has covered everything he needs to cover with him; I shared that I felt the same way. Scott is as encouraged as he has been and feels like his purpose in being with Daddy has been accomplished. I feel the same way completely. It was now time to rest.

CHAPTER 29

TUESDAY, DECEMBER 28

Lake Wobegon Days

Scott got away after breakfast this morning. I went by the nursing home around 11:45 to see Daddy. He is much the same. He was alert, but tearful. The nurse came with his Percocet. As he took it, I asked her about his morphine. He had it last at 10:00 this morning. She said that he was due for some, but the pharmacy was having trouble getting it today for some reason. She had a very small amount, but we decided to wait until he could take the full dose. He seemed to be in relative comfort, not wincing or making indications that he was in pain. I was concerned, however, that we get him pre-medicated before we tried to elevate his head so that he could eat. He was comfortable to wait, so we did. In the meantime, they brought his lunch: baked beans, butterscotch pudding, a hamburger with lettuce and tomato, water, tea and milk. He was able to pull himself more straight in the bed, giving me the "okay" sign that he was ready to eat. I elevated him just enough so that he could at least swallow his food without choking. He would eventually eat all of the beans, commenting, "I love those." He also drank all of the fluids and ate all of the pudding. Of the pudding, he stated, "That's so good, order me six more cans." His dentures bother him, so he told me to eat the hamburger, which I did.

I had talked to the hall nurse earlier about some of the issues discussed previously:

We may need to raise the dosage of his patch. (She said we would have to go from 50 to 75 mcg; it must be increased incrementally.)

The wound-care nurse would be by tomorrow to assess his wounds, probably making the changes that Scott had recommended.

The Hospice nurse was recommending something for anxiety. (I think that is a good idea.)

We should know about all of these issues soon.

Sammy called from his dental lab and talked with Daddy for at least 10 minutes. I told him that he was eating, but only the beans and pudding. Sammy offered to "bring my drill up there and trim his dentures," if that would help. Daddy simply does not want to wear them, but is happy to have soft, though not necessarily puréed, food. After they ended their conversation, Daddy told me that he didn't know that Robert Frederick, from Rose Hill, had died. Sammy had mentioned it on the phone. Daddy said that he knew him from "way back" when he lived in Rose Hill. He remembers him as a "good old boy." The news of Mr. Frederick stimulated him to talk about death. He said that he didn't need to worry about anything. I assured him that we were praying that God's grace would be sufficient. I also encouraged him to just "Relax and let us take care of you. We want to. God is helping, and is with, us all." He nodded and said, "You're right." We briefly discussed his conversation with Scott last night. He talked to me about how hard it is to let go. I again told him to relax. I reminded him that God's Spirit will sustain us all, to which he replied, "I know."

He remarked that he was satisfied that everything is working out just as it should and how gratifying it is for him to see "all of you youngins' working together. After all, we can't all 'peddle pills.'" I told him that each of us has a part to play and God is orchestrating everything. He smiled and closed his eyes, saying, "I am not afraid." I went to get us a cup of coffee from the break room on his hall. When I returned, he was sleeping peacefully. I stepped out to speak to the nurse. (The CNA had come by to tell us that she would be turning him in a little while.) I wanted to ask about the status of the morphine. The pharmacy is still expecting it soon, she confirmed. I told her that he appeared to be peaceful enough to be turned with out any "pre-medication," since the morphine was not presently available.

She told me that the 75 mcg. patch was approved. She also informed me that Daddy was going to be given Ativan for his anxiety, PRN (as needed). I asked her if he would have to ask for it. She said no, that the nurse would determine if he would need it or not. That sounded good to me. She also assured me that the wound-care nurse would be by tomorrow. Upon reflection, I feel that much good has been accomplished over the last couple of days, the mattress included.

Upon returning to his room, I found that he was still sleeping. He opened his eyes and said, "If I die today, at least I will be full and happy," as he smiled. I told him that today was not his day.

In a few moments, the CNA came back in to take his vitals, reposition and change him. I asked her about getting him soft food, but not puréed. She said she would tell the nurse. I also told her that we would like to possibly get him up for the worship service tomorrow. He gave the "okay" sign again. She said she was off tomorrow, but would pass on the information to the CNA who would be on duty.

One item that we did discuss as he was finishing his meal, but after Sammy had called, was the possibility of baptizing him. Daddy was very open and positive. I promised him that I would be discretionary as to when we might do it. (I will not do it in front of strangers nor at an inappropriate time.) He said to plan to do it and then said, "That's covered." It would certainly be an honor to do so for him. I told him that I would simply make the "sign of the cross" on his forehead with some water as I made the Trinitarian pronouncement. He seemed satisfied with that.

So for today, much has been accomplished:

The mattress is now in place.
He is on board to receive soft food.
He now has medication to help with his anxiety.
We anticipate changing therapy for his bedsores.
The patch will now be 75 mcg., an increase of 25 mcg.

* * *

Daddy seems to be at peace. I know that he is not completely out of pain and still cries; but he is at peace, at least from a philosophical and spiritual standpoint. He knows that he is dying and accepts that, though he struggles with the process of letting go. All of us would be the same way. I am beginning to realize that while encouraging him to talk more about that is probably a good thing, at the same time, it needs to be on his terms. He has talked through a great deal. There may be more to say about this process, but he seems to need support and encouragement most of all. While we must let him talk, we must also realize that talking can only take him...and us, so far.

He has talked through things with all of his children and I honestly feel that there are no longer any issues. He is afraid (is that even the best word?) of the process with its physical pain and letting go of what is familiar. He has already sampled what it is like to lose control of his cognitive abilities. The very real possibility that he will slip down that bank one more time, never to return, is unsettling to him, to say the least. There is nothing that we can do about it, other than to love and support him, and to be as near to him physically as we are able.

May God help us. "And God, help Daddy to remain 'as alert as he can, for as long as he can,' but no longer than is reasonable, considering the pain that he is in." Is tremendous pain a fair trade-off for times of lucidity? I don't know. In this case, only Daddy knows...and God.

* * *

When Cindy and I arrived to visit Daddy tonight, he was more or less as usual, for the last few days anyway. He was concerned about not being able to sort things out completely in his mind. This visit is a study in contrasts, in a limited way. For the first part of the visit, he was tearful and had a time getting it completely together, but by the end of our visit he seemed more himself. He also told me that he had a bad dream this afternoon, or was it? I know it was a dream, and so does Daddy, but he had a difficult time sorting it out completely.

He told me that he was in a house; a great, large, round room. He was in bed, just like he is now, and in tremendous pain. He saw all sorts of people there, some familiar, some not. He said that he cried out for two hours. Most ignored him, while some said they would help him later and left. No one ever did help him. He knows it was a dream, yet he also has trouble getting it clear in his mind. I feel sure it is his Alzheimer's.

As I was getting Daddy ready for his supper, David called. He could tell that Daddy was having more difficulty and that he isn't as well tonight. After Daddy and David talked, I talked with David. We ended our conversation with my encouraging him to close the store for a day or two if necessary so he can come and visit with Daddy. He said that there is a real possibility that he will close it Friday and come to see him, probably staying that night with us.

I think that Daddy's tearfulness and sadness are related just as much to his losing cognitive alertness as to the realization of his impending death. He cries because he knows that he is struggling to maintain his focus at times. It has to be a scary process going from times of relative clarity to times of unclear thinking and recognitions. Tonight, though, his tearfulness decreased as the time passed.

After the call ended, I warmed Daddy's tray and Cindy and I tried to get him ready for his supper. She warmed a towel in the sink for him to go over his face, which he did, while I put his food in the microwave. He had white beans as part of the meal. He joked about them and reminded me that he had pork and beans for lunch. He said, "I tell you right now, I'm not sure if this is going to work," as he laughed. He was beginning to feel better, although he would eventually not eat but one-half of the beans. The only other thing he ate was his entire cherry cobbler and I actually ended up feeding that to him. He would talk and take what seemed forever to get any of it eaten. We were not in a hurry, but I really wanted him to eat what he could. He loves cobbler, especially cherry. I told him that I loved it, too. As I fed him, he commented that I was "going to spoil" him. "I don't mind spoiling you a little bit," I assured him.

We didn't talk about a lot of heavy things tonight, simply enjoying each other's company. He brightened as the visit lengthened and had that relaxed, satisfied look on his face for much of it. I wish David could have called towards the end of the visit; he would have been more encouraged, I am sure.

Daddy told me that Harold had called. Harold did call while I was there, talking to me and telling me he had called earlier today, but forgot to tell Daddy something. He said to tell Daddy that "Today was the 18th anniversary." I told Daddy and he said that Harold had been sober for 18 years. (I had guessed that was what Harold meant.) Daddy has obviously helped Harold so much and he can be very proud. I am proud of Daddy for giving to others the way that he does.

We talked about the roll Daddy had with his supper. It brought his mind to the time that he was at *UNC*. He told me that when he worked in the cafeteria at the school, he would sometimes get some of the rolls and butter from the kitchen. They were "absolutely delicious!" He didn't get butter at home very much. The school would make the rolls on racks that would "fill this room." He also talked about the biscuits his mother would make. She would put them in the "safe," or cabinet. He would leave school (*UNC*) for home and would often not get a meal until he got to the house. He would get a biscuit, and maybe a cold piece of chicken if he was really fortunate. He would put molasses in the biscuit, or whatever else he could find. I told him that I had eaten Grandma's biscuits as a child myself, to which he replied, "You know what I'm talking about." The conversation brought a smile to his face.

After a while, he said that he was getting sleepy. He told us that he enjoyed our visit, saying it was "rewarding" and "very peaceful." He said he loved to visit without hurry and just talking about whatever came to mind. I wish he could always feel this way. If he dies tonight, I believe he would die at peace. I think he has reached the point where he will have good days and bad days, or in this case, perhaps good hours and bad hours. May we take advantage of these "good hours."

I asked him if he was okay for us to leave, and he said that he was. We called for his medicine. He took the Percocet, the Ativan and the morphine without any hesitation or problem. After his medication, I took his hand and asked if we could pray. He said "Sure," so I took his right hand in both of mine while Cindy and I prayed with him.

As I prepared to leave, I asked him if he would like to listen to the "Lake Wobegon" CD Sammy had left him. He said he would so I took the player and CD from the drawer and got it ready for him. Once I had him situated, I asked him if it was all right to which he smiled and gave me the "okay" sign. I hit the pause button so I could tell him I love him and kiss him goodbye. He readily accepted our show of affection, though he did tell me to "Hit that button" to make the CD resume. I asked him if the volume was good. He smiled and again gave me the "okay" sign. He gives the "okay" sign a lot, now that I think of it. I will *always* associate it with him.

As we began to leave, he appeared quite content, eyes closed and a smile on his face. I left the *UNC-UNCW* basketball game on very low volume while he listened to Garrison Keeler. It is an image that I hope I will never forget, for it was the picture of contentment.

CHAPTER 30

WEDNESDAY, DECEMBER 29

Contentment and Distress

I *haven't been to see Daddy yet, but have been thinking about him this morning. As I reflect on all that has transpired, I wonder just how much he has known leading up to this point? Is it possible that he knew for certain that Alzheimer's was going to progressively overcome him? Did he have a diagnosis at some point that clearly revealed his disease earlier? Or, if no diagnosis had been given, did he come to realize that he was having times of mental difficulty? Or did he know, but hid it from us? Is that why he got his affairs in order the first week of October, i. e. a living will and trust? Did he come to High Point for rehabilitation, but in reality thought that he may have to stay as his Alzheimer's got worse? We know that he was diagnosed with Alzheimer's, or told about his disease, while in Lumberton, but he downplayed it, even joking about it and how obvious it was that he didn't have Alzheimer's.*

He had been going to Duke in years past, dealing with prostate related issues. While I first heard about his Alzheimer's at his hospital stay in Lumberton last month, did he know more? Did he want to get things settled because of sure knowledge, or simply strong intuition and the realization that mentally he was having times of difficulty? The falls that he has suffered over the last few years, were they related to Alzheimer's? While we will never know the answers to these questions for sure, I feel confident that God brought him to this point in his life in order to prepare him for eternity and also to prepare us for his impending death. God's grace continues to be nothing short of amazing.

But my mind goes back to Venice, Italy, seven or eight years ago. I remember very vividly that he was almost like he has been recently when we arrived in Italy after a long trip with very little rest. He became disoriented that evening, talking "out of his head." I remember helping him get dressed for bed and the way that he honestly didn't know where he was for a time. I had told Cindy about it soon after. Was it fatigue, or Alzheimer's? Again, we will never know, but I have my strong suspicions. Alzheimer's can take a good while to fully manifest itself and sufferers can hide it for a time. Daddy has proven over the years that he can hide things when he needs to do so. I can only wonder how long he has really been dealing with this.

* * *

As I arrived at the nursing home for his lunch today, I found Daddy with a glassy look on his face, not able to complete his thoughts and very tearful. I asked him how he was and as usual his response was, "I'm okay." I asked him if he knew who I was; he responded blandly, "Roland," and began to cry. I tried to help him with his lunch, but he only ate about one-fourth of it. He took his morphine at 12:30. I was to find out that he had not taken any since last night, and that he continues to reject it when they bring it. He had not taken any Ativan either.

They brought him some Ensure in a small cup and he drank it down with no problem, stating, "We want that every time." He told me how good it was for him to take it regularly. He is aware that he needs the nutrition it provides. *Hospice* would also tell us later today that Ensure could literally replace a meal, if necessary.

Carol, Mike, Ashly and Sammy (her husband) arrived while the wound care nurse was beginning to assess Daddy. The door was pulled to and the curtain drawn, but Carol came in and stood with us as the nurse gave the update. Daddy's wounds are serious. She said:

His bedsores are actually larger than when he arrived in High Point.

They are not responding to the present treatment.

We can try other mediations and therapies, just as Scott has suggested.

Daddy may need to go to the wound care center. Dr. Shull, from our church, is a surgeon and serves on staff at the facility.

After she finished, we talked. Daddy spoke about the significance of helping others and how everyone has a role to play. (His morphine was relieving his pain; he was more coherent.) He said, "It makes more sense to give something to somebody with three kids who need it, than to give it to somebody whose kid already has three tricycles in the back yard." Beyond a doubt, Daddy has helped more people than we will ever know.

I called Dr. Shull's wife Marie, who works with volunteer ministries at our church. She said that he was out of town today, but he would look at Daddy personally before the church board meeting tomorrow night. I gave her my contact numbers and thanked her for her help. The *Hospice* nurse would later comment that she did not know of anyone else who actually got a visit from the doctor himself; we are truly blessed to have Daddy here.

Another blessing is the wound care nurse. As she talked in the hall with Carol and me today after examining Daddy, she told us that she, her husband and daughter pray every night together. They always pray for God's healing to be on the facility and are especially praying for our father. Her eyes became moist with tears as she spoke. Carol and I both gave her a "group hug." Again, God's mercy and grace have simply been astounding.

The *Hospice* nurse came at 4:00 to give Daddy "the once over" as he described it. She had several things to say. She was a retired nurse, very compassionate and caring, with a sense of humor. After she finished, Daddy began telling her about his trips to Europe. He was very alert and animated as he told her that Ashly would have some information mailed to her if she would leave her address with her. She wrote it down and gave it to Ashly and soon left the room. It was a very productive meeting. Among other things, the *Hospice* nurse shared the following items:

She is not sure that the trauma of moving him to the wound care center, even for a day visit, would be worth it.

The fact that Dr. Shull is coming is a plus. He may be able to do something in the room itself. We will just have to wait and see. Daddy needs to eat and drink, especially the Ensure.

She had been in almost all of the facilities in the area, and ours is one of the best.

Daddy really needs to take his morphine.

She told him, and us, that pain could be a much greater distraction than any side effects he may have from the medications. (It was obvious that the morphine was helping him as she talked.) She told him that we want to enjoy this time with him and when he is in pain that is not possible. Also, when a person is in pain, they cannot talk, they cannot eat, and they cannot interact in a constructive way. "Take the morphine when it is offered." She did not adjust his medication amounts or frequencies today.

After she left the room, I asked if I might speak to her. I asked how long he might live, based on her experience. While she did not give a certain time, she did say that "Overall, he is in pretty good shape." However, she was concerned about his blood pressure since it was only 86/20. His heart rate was 109. Rapid heart rate can indicate that the cancer is active. She stressed the importance of the things that we had discussed with Daddy and said that she would be back next Wednesday. I thanked her as she left.

* * *

I went back at supper. Carol, Mike, Ashly and Sammy had left earlier this afternoon. Daddy was making fairly good progress on his supper, eating beef and noodles. He was talkative and alert (as he is *most* evenings). He was somewhat slumped down in the bed, however. I asked him if he would like to be adjusted and he said, "Yes." I called for help and they had him more comfortable in just a few minutes. He has two "looks" I am discovering:

He sometimes has a look of contentment when he is in minor pain. During those times, he is smiling and comfortable.

Other times he has a look of distress when he is in significant pain. He has a glassy look and is obviously very uncomfortable.

Tonight was a strong look of contentment. He had taken his morphine just as we had stressed to him this afternoon…and it shows.

He said that we had accomplished a lot today and that he felt very "happy" with the current situation. He is glad that Dr. Shull is coming tomorrow. The two major issues, at least at this point, are pain management and treatment options for the bedsores. We have addressed them both today. As we talked, he was alert and eating on his own.

David called and Daddy talked to him. They had a fairly coherent conversation. David is coming Friday and Saturday and he and Lynda plan to spend the night with us. As they talked, I went to warm Daddy's food.

As he ate, I spoke to his nurse, expressing how much better Daddy gets along when his pain is under control. I told her that he is "so much better" during those times and that his cognitive alertness is at 90 to 95%. She said they would do all that they can. I thanked her and went back to the room.

Daddy had eaten a decent amount and wanted to work on his cake. He ate one-third of it in one bite and smiled. He would finish the cake and seemed quite content and satisfied. We watched *Gunsmoke* as he gradually finished his meal. He asked Cindy about her parents and eventually talked about "Cousin Dolly;" she was Sandra's grandmother. He told us that used to you would visit people because you wanted to, not because of obligation. Also, people would always offer you something, just because you were "company," even if it was just a "biscuit and cheese." He was very content as he reminisced.

As we talked, I reminded him yet again how important it is that he take his pain medications, especially the morphine. I told him that I want him to be able to talk to me and that he is clearer when he takes it. "I don't like coming in and finding you like you were this morning." In my mind, at least for now, pain affects him as much, or maybe more, than Alzheimer's. It seems to me that times of intense pain bring on Alzheimer's type symptoms, whereas the easing of his pain keeps him more comfortable...and clear. He agreed with my assessment of the situation.

He was growing tired, but before we got him settled ("No Lake Wobegon tonight"), Marlena, whose mother is a resident across the hall, came by. She has been so good to Daddy, and supportive of us. She shook his hand and commented on his nails, offering to trim them. I told her that we had just asked *Hospice* about that today and they said that it was fine to trim them, but we need to make sure he doesn't get cut in the process. She told us that she was a "licensed manicurist" and could use the file to get them in shape. It was another answer to prayer! Though simple, it shows God's concern for even the little things in our lives.

We lowered him all the way down, and he was soon asleep. He asked me to turn out the lights before I left. We exchanged "I love you(s)." Cindy and I left him sleeping peacefully; I pray he can remain that way.

CHAPTER 31

THURSDAY, DECEMBER 30

God Has Worked Everything Out

After some lunch, Cindy and I went to visit Daddy. Although his lunch had arrived, he was not eating. It was still on the table near the bed, but was not prepared for him to eat. I went to his side, noticing that he was in some pain, yet thinking clearly; he was wet with sweat. I asked him if he was hot as I turned down the thermostat on the window heater. Cindy went to get a cloth soaked in cool water. She brought it and I began to wipe his head and face with the cloth as we talked.

He told me that he had a temperature when it was checked earlier; it had been 100.1. I later found out that it was actually 100.7. They will automatically send him to the Emergency Room if it hits 101. I felt of his forehead and face. He felt a little clammy, but not warm. He told me that he did not feel like he had a fever. I went to ask the CNA about Daddy's most recent vitals. She informed me that he showed a temperature earlier, that she wasn't sure what it was but would check on it. I told her knowing it was up, but under 101, was sufficient for the moment. I knew that he was not at 101 because he had not been sent to the hospital.

Returning to his room, the nurse brought his morphine, which he readily accepted. After a few minutes, he ate a little beans and rice and another vegetable. He also ate about one-half of his Jell-O and drank all of his milk and tea. We sort of recapped where we are:

Hospice visit yesterday, Dr. Shull coming today, Sammy and Sandra tonight and David and Lynda Friday night. He was very alert and showed a smile a few times, but was still in some pain. He complained to Cindy and me that his right side hurt him the most. At one point he remarked, "I know what it is, but why bother about it at this point." I did not make any comment.

As he was finishing what he would eat today, someone from Lumberton called. She had been a customer for 30 years according to Daddy. She was asking to speak to him, but he did not feel like talking, so she quizzed me about the length of time that he has left and asked exactly who I was, anyway. Eventually, she took down some general directions to the nursing home and we hung up. I went back to feeding Daddy. (He was basically done.) I told him about the potential visit and he simply groaned. His morphine was beginning to kick in.

James Smith, one of the chaplains from our church, came by and had a good visit with Daddy. I expressed to him how much I appreciated his visit, even though it was his day to make calls at the nursing home.

After he left, I checked Daddy's temperature with the ther-mometer *Hospice* leaves in their notebook. His temperature was 98.5. I asked the nurse if we should do something, seeing that he was running a fever earlier. She said that at 101, he goes to the Emergency Room (I already knew that) and that his temperature earlier was 100.7 (I did not know that at the time.) They brought him Tylenol, changed and turned him. She expressed concern for his bedsores if he left the nursing home, saying that the hospital could not take as good a care of them as the nursing home could, in her opinion. I did not comment, but do remember that he got excellent care at the hospital a couple of weeks ago.

After they were finished with him, we went back into the room. He was on his left side facing the door. While his pain had eased earlier, he was now somewhat uncomfortable again and looked sleepy. I told him to rest if he could, and that I would be back this evening. He responded groggily, "I think I can sleep." Cindy and I left the room after a prayer together with him, asking for God's strength and peace.

I wonder what the immediate future holds. I am concerned that he has run a temperature, even though he doesn't seem to have one at this time. If he gets an infection, will he recover from it? Why had his temperature gone up earlier today? This evening, I plan to find out what his vitals have been this afternoon. I would have called Hospice if his temperature had not improved. I pray that it is simply a "fluke."

* * *

Cindy and I went to the nursing home for Daddy's supper. Sammy, Sandra, Vada and Austin were there. Daddy had eaten his supper, about 80%, according to Sammy. He was drinking coffee, with Sammy's assistance. He looked fairly alert, but was clearly uncomfortable. After greeting everyone, I stepped out to find out about Daddy's temperature. He has not had a fever since this morning; that is good. I told Sammy about the fever this morning and the update just now. We are cautious but not overly concerned.

In a few minutes, Dr. Shull, and his wife Marie, came by to check on Daddy. They stepped in and we all were introduced. Everyone went out and waited in the hall while he examined Daddy. In a short time, he came out and asked me if he should speak to Sammy and me alone, or the whole crowd. We all heard what he had to say about the bedsores, except Marie, who waited in the hall. He said:

Daddy's sores are bad, but have not reached the point where they are "dry," like a scab.

When they reach that point, he will need to go into the hospital for a "few days." We want to wait until they reach the point where it is necessary. He is not a wound care candidate at this time. The hospital stay would be necessary because of his condition, but would be traumatic and "wear him out" according to Dr. Shull.

Dr. Shull will personally keep an eye on the wounds every four to five days and keep me updated on any changes and recommendations that he might make.

He will be in touch with Dr. Orr, the nursing home physician, to see about taking Daddy on as his personal patient,

195

also recommending some changes to the medications and/or bandages used.

After some encouraging words, he and Marie left. I think we were all encouraged by the fact that the doctor himself was going to see to Daddy's bedsores, and not just his nurse or assistant. Daddy was alert and able to understand what was said. He seemed to be encouraged as well. The wound care situation is under control; I am very pleased.

David, and then Scott, called. Daddy spoke with them both in turn and I also filled them in as well as I could. They were both pleased with the way the bedsore situation is being handled. I would call Carol later this evening and update her. It now seems that everyone is on the same page, relative to his wound care.

Daddy had been moved after Dr. Shull examined him earlier. He was now on his left side and in great pain. They adjusted him but his pain was still significant. I called *Hospice* and told the nurse on call that he was in pain. She told us to switch the Ativan to be *scheduled* every six hours instead of PRN (as needed). She said that it would help to relax his smooth muscles and also help the pain medications to work better. Since his pain was so severe, we made the decision to begin the Ativan at 12:00 midnight, giving it to him every six hours. The nurse also informed us that it would allow us some room to adjust the other pain medications, if the Ativan worked well. We will try.

By 7:45, Daddy had relaxed and was ready to lie down. He asked us to turn out the light, but before I did so, I asked him if we might have prayer. We all held hands as I prayed for him and the family. I prayed for God's strength and peace to be with him. I prayed the same for our family and especially asked God to grant safety to David and Lynda as they come tomorrow. I also asked for safety for Sammy and his family as they go home tomorrow. After our prayer, Daddy said, "God has worked everything out."

He has had morphine at 12:30, 3:00, 5:00 and 7:00. He was peaceful and ready to lie down. We got him settled, turned out the lights and left him peacefully. It was a very good visit.

CHAPTER 32

FRIDAY, DECEMBER 31

A Spiritual Butterfly

Sammy, his family, Cindy and I arrived around lunch for a visit. Daddy was very uncomfortable and in substantial pain. I checked with the nurse and discovered that he had not had morphine for several hours. They had found him sleeping and did not want to wake him. They need to give him the morphine, however, even if they have to wake him up; he needs to stay ahead of the pain. *Hospice* has stressed the need for him to receive the morphine on a regular basis and not get behind.

I had the nurse give him his morphine and Ativan. Sammy, Sandra, Cindy and I wiped Daddy's face and brow with a warm, damp cloth. He was not running a fever, but was clammy and sweating significantly. We talked to him and held his hands. He would manage to get out a word or two, but nothing very concrete. Again, he was very uncomfortable and not coherent.

Having taken the morphine and Ativan, he eventually began to settle down. He drank some Ensure, as well as an orange juice-like formula that has protein and other things to aid in the healing of his bedsores. He called for coffee, drinking about one-half of the cup. He did not eat any lunch. It appears that he has taken a clear turn downward, but it is hard to say. It seems obvious, however, to me.

Early in the afternoon, Daddy had company from Fayetteville. He was not up to visitors, but they were kind and courteous. She and Daddy had worked together in Whiteville while at "Simmons' Drug Store." Simmons' had two stores in Whiteville. Daddy did relief work at both when he lived there in the 70s and early 80s. Even though that was 25 years ago, she said she still calls on Daddy for help about any questions she has about medications. She also has lost a daughter to cancer. Her daughter was only 48 and actually very healthy, having run the New York City Marathon. She died from a brain tumor. They continued to visit with Daddy while I went out to the "patio" near the TV room; Sammy and Vada were there.

He asked me what funeral home would pick up Daddy after his death. I told him that *Cumby's* on Eastchester Drive, here in High Point, would be who takes care of the body. We also talked about the headstone and what would be on it. I reminded him that Daddy has requested, "But the best of all is, God is with us," a quote from John Wesley, be on it. I will get it to him in writing when the time comes. In a few minutes, Sammy went back in while Sandra, Cindy and Austin came outside.

We talked about what seems to be happening to Daddy. Sandra made the comment that it is almost as if Daddy is in a "cocoon," struggling to get out. But he will eventually escape, turning into a "spiritual butterfly." As far as I know, that sums it up pretty well.

The focus of our discussion turned to how we are responding emotionally to all that is taking place. I told Sandra that I had not really cried for four or five days. I think I am subconsciously "keeping it together" until the funeral is over. Keeping this journal certainly helps me to deal with the situation as well.

Today has not been a good day for Daddy. He eventually settled down, nevertheless, and was actually sleeping when we went back into his room. He didn't say anything, but would respond weakly to questions or comments and look around as if in a daze. The Ativan and morphine have certainly relaxed him. As we left him, we turned the radio to a "timeless classics" station; Daddy likes that type of music. They play Sinatra, Dean Martin, Patsy Cline and everything in between. He obviously is not interested in, or up to, watching television. The radio seemed more appropriate; he did not seem to mind.

As we were leaving, he smiled and reached out his hands as if to grasp something. When I asked him if he was dreaming, he opened his eyes and said, "Yes." I said that it must be a good dream. He smiled again. *"Lord, help him to have good dreams and not bad."*

We left to get some lunch. Cindy, Vada, Austin and I went to a nearby *Wendy's*. We brought Sandra something back; Sammy was not hungry.

* * *

When I arrived back at the nursing home, Daddy did not seem to be in pain. He was making a lot of hand motions and not very talkative or alert. He would ask for water occasionally, or say something unintelligible. He mentioned "John Henry" once, a person I do not know. Could he be starting to see people who are gone on already? There is no way to know what the images or thoughts are that are passing through his mind at this point.

Sammy and I talked about the potential need to bring in *Hospice* to check Daddy's present condition. I told him that I did not want to call them too early, but want to do so at the most appropriate time, if possible. I also told him that I would wait until this evening and then play it by ear as to whether we should call or not. Sammy said that he knows this could be the last time that he sees Daddy, but he is okay with that. He does not feel compelled to be here at the actual moment of his death, but would like to be called if we are given a certain timeframe that Daddy might have left to live. I assured him that I would call all of Daddy's children *if* we were given a fairly good indication of his estimated time of death.

David called this afternoon, informing us that Lynda has been sick today. They are delaying their trip to High Point until tomorrow. I told Daddy and he seemed to understand what I was trying to tell him and accepting of it. Shortly thereafter, Vada, Sandra, Austin, Cindy and I went to our house for supper. We had a "big breakfast," including sausage, grits and eggs. *I wish Daddy were here to enjoy it.*

We went back to be with Sammy and sit with Daddy around 6:30. Daddy was sleeping *very* soundly. They came in to turn him and he did not even wake up. I'm not sure if it is the Ativan or the morphine, or both, but he is more or less "knocked out" at this point. We are a bit concerned because we want him to be as alert as possible, even if he is not able to talk very much. I suggested to Sammy that we should contact *Hospice* again and see about adjusting his medication. Perhaps he should only get .25 mg. of the Ativan, instead of the .5 mg. Eventually, we settled on leaving it at .5, but changed it back to PRN (as needed), rather than scheduled, up to .5 mg. every six hours. We also decided to skip the 12:00 dose coming up tonight. He took the 6:00 dose while I was gone to supper. The *Hospice* nurse suggested that we not give him the morphine at this point, unless he stirs. While we do want to "stay ahead of the pain," we want to be careful to not over-medicate him. He is heavily medicated at this juncture. Also, morphine suppresses the respiratory system. I asked the nurse to keep an eye on Daddy and give him his morphine if he showed the slightest sign that he may be in pain. He assured me that he would do so.

Returning to the room, Sammy and I found Daddy still resting soundly and peacefully. We left his radio on, and the TV, with the volume all the way down. We also left the light over the head of the bed on, not the "reading" light, but the one that illuminates the ceiling. We left him in peace.

As we exited the building, Sammy and Vada walked ahead of us. Once outside, Vada cried openly. This whole experience is very trying, both physically and emotionally. We *all* need a special touch of God's grace. We plan to go back in the morning.

Arriving at our house, we spent a period of time watching the New Year's Marathon of *The Three Stooges*. We all needed the distraction after such an emotionally draining day. I also could not help but think that *if* Daddy survives tonight, 2005 will find him living into a new year. I am fully confident and 100% sure this will be his last year on *this* earth.

He lived to the age of 77, born on October 21, 1927 and will die in 2005; I am accepting of that fact. I will inform David, Carol and Scott about the medication adjustments tomorrow. I have to believe that they will accept whatever I think is best for Daddy and that my judgment is sound. Someone has to be Daddy's advocate and I consider it an honor to have the responsibility. Again, he has told me several times that he is depending on me to be just that.

With God's help, I will not let him down.

ACT 3
JANUARY

CLOSING THE SCENE

It's sad when our daddies die. Makes us one less person inside.

—Pamela Ribon

CHAPTER 33

SATURDAY, JANUARY 1

See You Soon

S ammy and his family. along with Cindy and me, went back to the nursing home for Daddy's lunch. He was actually alert, relatively speaking. He was not in pain as far as we could tell; he had an Ativan at 6:00 this morning. We talked to the nurse about his pain situation. For the present we would like to keep him as alert as we can, but still want to do whatever is necessary to control his pain. She asked if we wanted the morphine given and we acknowledged that it would probably be best. We still want to stay ahead of the pain if at all possible. She would bring it in just a few minutes, which she did. He is now off the Percocet, but is on the patch (75 mcg.) and 5 to 10 ccs of morphine, orally every two hours, as needed.

His lunch soon arrived, including black-eyed peas and greens, traditional New Year's foods. They are supposed to bring good luck, but I do not believe in it. Daddy, however, can use all of the good things that he can get right now. If it includes luck, then we will take it. I got the tray ready by mashing the peas up with the fork. He also had a piece of cornbread. Sandra recommended putting some milk on it, which I did. I have heard Daddy speak about eating milk and cornbread when he was growing up as a child. I turned the feeding process over to Sammy. Daddy ate some of it and actually seemed to enjoy it. He also ate a very small taste of his brownie. He is having a good day, but it seems to me that he is clearly not eating as much as he has previously. He may be taking another turn, *but today is a good day* and I want to enjoy it with both him and the family. He did eat well at breakfast, we were told.

He became more alert as his lunch was fed to him. It was clear, however, that he is still not as cognizant as he should be. I don't think he is totally aware of what is going on, but simply enjoying the experience. We are in the period where alertness is still a desirable thing. Finding the balance though, between alertness and pain management, is still *one* of the biggest challenges that we are facing. I'm constantly reminded of Daddy's statement to me, on more than one occasion, "I want to remain as alert as I can for as long as I can." I intend to keep him that way (and so does the entire family I'm sure) for as long as is *reasonably* possible.

After eating, Daddy responded to questions with very short answers. He would also make exclamatory remarks such as, "Oh boy!" or "Oh my!" regularly. He did not say them as if he was in pain, but rather as if to say, "Well, here we are at this point and I am reasonably comfortable." Sammy found Daddy's glasses and asked him if he wanted them on. Daddy was affirmative. When they were placed on him, he exclaimed, "Oh my!" rather loudly, as if to acknowledge that he could indeed see so much better. We all laughed at his amazement; it was funny. I am so glad to know that we can still see the humor in the midst of his suffering. It is not easy, but you have to have those times when you "let off some steam" as it were.

We decided, since Daddy was having such a good day, to call Marlena. She had given us her number and instructed us to call her when he was having a good day so that she could do his nails. I got her voice mail and left a message, telling her that she could use her own discretion about an appropriate time to do them. She has been so kind to Daddy, even though her own mother suffers from a stroke.

As we got ready to go, I stepped back into the room alone. Daddy said something that sounded like Italian. I asked him what it meant; he said, "See you soon." I replied, "I'll see *you* soon," and left.

Sammy and his family left when we did, around 1:30. He was very distraught. I asked him if I could do anything. He said that he felt it was the last time he would see Daddy. At this time, I feel that

Daddy will be here on Wednesday (the day Sammy plans to return), but cannot be sure, of course.

It has to be hard on my other siblings to be such a distance away. I can be at Daddy's side in less than 10 minutes, whereas they must travel over three hours, or more in Scott's case. While I am worn out from being with him so much, they are distressed over having to leave him. I still know in my heart of hearts that God has worked things out so that Daddy is right where he should be. I cannot feel bad about the effect his decision to stay in High Point is having on the other children. It was <u>his</u> decision and I am convinced that God's hand was, and is, in that decision. I have not felt, furthermore, <u>any</u> negativity from them. To a person, we all want what is totally best for Daddy.

* * *

I went back to the nursing home around supper. David and Lynda had arrived; Daddy was still smiling and obviously not in any pain. He had eaten some supper, *very* little actually. Lynda did feed him some chocolate candy. It was fairly messy and we all laughed about the dirty face that he had. He also chose a cup of applesauce and a container of orange juice from the "evening cart" that comes by occasionally offering refreshments to the residents. Mike and Carol had arrived by this time and she fed him the apple-sauce, which he seemed to enjoy very much. He would only take a couple of sips of his orange juice. He ate all of his applesauce though. He has not had any Ativan today, but has taken his morphine with regularity. He is still somewhat alert and seems quite comfortable. It has been a good day for him, both alert and free of pain. It is the first day since his arrival in High Point that he has gone the entire day in relative comfort.

We talked about the horn on the windowsill that Sammy had brought. It is an instrument, made from a bull's horn, which Granddaddy Roland used to call his dogs when he went hunting. Carol asked what it was as we handed it to Daddy, and he tried to explain it. He then attempted to blow it, but used the wrong end of it first. I turned it the correct way and he made several good efforts to blow it again, but could not get the desired sound. However, we all enjoyed his attempt very much. I think every single person was smiling.

Carol, Mike, Cindy and I prepared to leave together. They would spend the night with us. On the way out, we spoke to the nurse, reminding her that we did not want the Ativan given unless it was clearly needed. We stressed, however, that she should not hesitate to give it if he seemed to need it. We were all on the same page.

Before leaving, I told Daddy that I loved him. I asked him if he loved me. He said, "Most of the time." We all laughed. I then asked him if that should go in my journal. His response, "Just put the positive." It was funny and an obvious attempt at humor on his part. He still tries to find the humorous side of things.

Carol, Mike, Cindy and I went to eat supper at the *Rainbow Restaurant* near the nursing home; it was about 8:00. After our meal, we went home to our house to rest.

CHAPTER 34

SUNDAY, JANUARY 2

Trying to Die

After dropping Cindy off at our church, I parked the car. Carol called my cell phone before I got out of the car informing me that she had received a call at our house from the nursing home. Daddy refuses to eat. When they last gave him his morphine he took his finger and pushed it out of his mouth. Is he trying to tell us that he is tiring of the struggle? He has been through so much. I know his pain is increasing. Perhaps he is trying to tell us in actions what he now finds impossible to tell us verbally, "I am in pain and do not want to continue the way that I am currently going." I'm not sure, but it is just a thought. He is also calling out "Mama," Carol said. I know that in the later stages of the dying process, persons who have died can sometimes be "seen" by the dying person. Is Daddy beginning to see family members who have gone on before?

Carol told me that she and Mike are going to see Daddy when they leave our house. David and Lynda may be on the way to see him from the hotel where they stayed last night. I would go to church and told Carol that my cell phone would be off, but that she could page me if an emergency occurs with Daddy. I would know that I needed to go to the nursing home if her cell number appears on the pager. She said that she felt they could handle it, but the nurse suggested that they find something Daddy likes to eat and put his medications in that. He is refusing *anything* by mouth and seems to be in intense pain.

"Lord, help Daddy."

* * *

After church, Cindy and I went immediately to the nursing home. Daddy was actually resting. David and Lynda were there along with Mike and Carol. David had been able to talk Daddy into taking his morphine. His blood pressure had been checked and was low; his pulse is now at 120. He also had taken one other medication besides the morphine. It was given because he complained of nausea and feeling sick at his stomach.

By the time we arrived, he appeared to me to be virtually nonresponsive, in a "sleep state," semi comatose. His mouth was open; his eyes were just open at times. He would look around the room, but as if he does not really see us. It is as if he is seeing, yet *not* seeing. I am sure he can hear us, but am not convinced that he is conscious of what is happening around him, or of who is present in the room.

Mr. Lowry, who has worked faithfully at the drug store, and Sandra, who works there as well, came to see Daddy. Sandra has visited one other time. It is the first time that Mr. Lowry has visited him. Daddy thinks a lot of them both. When he was able to talk on the phone, he would always talk to them both, even if he could not talk to others because he was simply too weak or in so much pain. It encourages me to know that they would come all the way from Lumberton just to visit Daddy.

With the change in Daddy we felt that *Hospice* should be called. Eventually, the *Hospice* nurse came and examined him, stating that he was "very comfortable," suggesting that we give the morphine by a dropper since he was clearly having difficulty swallowing. Morphine can be readily absorbed either behind the back, bottom teeth, or under the tongue. At this point, he could potentially choke if it is given in a cup, as he has been receiving it. I asked her if a morphine injection was a possibility. Her response was, "I really don't think that it will be necessary." She said to call her if he has further issues with pain management, telling us that the nursing home staff can do all that is necessary to keep him comfortable at this point. She also told me, when I asked her, that the nursing home can make the pronouncement of death. Do all that we can to keep him comfortable, tell him that we love him and are near, since "The hearing is the last thing to go." *I've always wondered how they know that.*

She also told us to go ahead and put him on oxygen. It will not prolong his life, obviously, but will help him to be more comfortable. We put him on oxygen, the tube, not the mask. His vital signs at 2:00 today, according to the *Hospice* nurse are: blood pressure-67/30, heart rate is 118 and his temperature is 99.1. It had been over 100 earlier today, but he seems to be cooling some. His forehead and arms are clammy, but his feet and toes are still warm.

Before she left, we thanked her. We also showed her several pictures in the room, each of us speaking about what they were of, and the occasion involved. She stepped out and the others (Carol, Mike, David, Lynda, Mr. Lowry and Sandra) followed. I think we all needed a break, perhaps, after the sobering news. Cindy and I were the last to go out of the room. I took his right hand, rubbed his right forearm and whispered in his ear (as he faced the window), "Daddy, we are all here. I love you." Very faintly, he said into my right ear, "I love you." I asked Cindy if she had heard it, telling her, "He said that he loved me." I got emotional, not believing what had just happened. What a tremendous gift God has given Daddy, and us, in having this time together with him...and with one another.

The *Hospice* nurse was in the hall. I asked her if we should call in the rest of the family; she said that was a good idea, but stressed that we do not know how long he has left. She did say "He is trying to die, but he is very comfortable." I told the family later that I wanted to baptize Daddy; he and I had discussed it earlier. They all felt that it was a good idea, though I am not sure when I will do so.

* * *

Carol and Mike left for a while. Cindy and I went to my office. She called her parents, updating them, while I did some preliminary work on his funeral. I cannot believe that the time is actually drawing so near. While I am honored to do it, I know that it will be very hard. It is a promise I made, however, to Daddy. By God's grace, I hope to keep it.

I ran off the scripture with which I plan to open the service. It is from 2 Corinthians 4 and 5, the same passage Sammy referenced in a card he had sent Daddy. I have read it to Daddy two or three times. I also got the Committal together, ran it off and put it in the small black notebook that I use for such occasions. I picked up the file containing items that I have been collecting ever since I began to sense that Daddy's condition was terminal, even before December 9, the day that his cancer was confirmed. I also took the general funeral folder that I use. Having eaten something from *Wendy's* earlier in Daddy's room (Mike and Carol had brought Cindy and me something), we went back to the nursing home. It was 4:30.

* * *

Carol and Mike had returned. David and Lynda were still there also. I felt that I should call Sammy. He is planning to come Wednesday, but may come Tuesday; he is not quiet sure. It is evident that everyone is struggling over how to work out their comings and goings. We are not sure of Daddy's status relative to his actual time of death. I can certainly understand the dilemma that the other children are facing.

Mike and Carol soon left, but she is coming back tomorrow, following Mike to Raleigh (to work) and continuing on to High Point from there. She said that she plans to stay at least a couple of nights, perhaps longer, if necessary. She wants to "give (me) a break." I feel tired, but know that I want to be near him regardless of who is here. We have reached a critical hour, I think.

I called Scott, filling him in on the details about Daddy. He asked me to call him in the morning and give him an update as to how things go tonight. I promised him that I would call him when I go by early tomorrow to see Daddy. While we know that Daddy is having difficulty swallowing, I might try to get him to eat a little, depending on how I find him then.

Around 6:30, I sensed strongly that we should go ahead and baptize Daddy. I asked David what he thought. He said, "Let's do it." I had brought *The Discipline of the Wesleyan Church* with me from the office earlier today. It had been on the stand beside Daddy's bed. David and Lynda stood on Daddy's right, near the window while I stood on his left. I retrieved a cup of water from his nightstand, as well as *The Discipline*. After reading the statement from *The Discipline* (turning the questions there into statements since Daddy could not respond to a question), I spoke the words as an affirmation of Daddy's faith, which I *know* that he has. I then dipped my finger into the water and made the pronouncement, "Samuel MacDonald Cavanaugh, I baptize you in the name of the Father, and of the Son and of the Holy Spirit," making the sign of the cross on his forehead. We closed with prayer. As David came and stood beside me, I told him that we had taken Daddy as far as we could; now we have to leave him in God's care. He agreed. We were both crying. As I held Daddy's left hand and rubbed his forearm, I was amazed at the thought of him receiving baptism *and* communion in these last days of his life. God has certainly been good to us all.

David and Lynda finally began to prepare to leave around 7:20. It was very hard for David. He cried openly as we walked with them to the end of the hall to go outside. He struggled over whether to leave or not. I told him that Daddy could be like this for several days (I do not think he will, but obviously have no way of knowing for sure.) He told me that in his "heart of hearts" he knew Daddy would want the store to be open. David said that Daddy had often told him, "Those people are depending on us." They get their medications on the first of the month and need them. "We have an obligation to them." I told David to feel good about leaving, affirming that is what Daddy would want him to do. I also told him, "I hope you have the biggest day you have ever had." (They would indeed have the biggest day in the history of the store on Monday.) He said that Daddy would live on in our hearts and our "memories." I agreed, but reminded him that Daddy would live on *literally* after death, in God's presence. He would die here, but immediately be alive in God's presence. After some more crying and embracing, he and Lynda left. It was a very hard thing to take...

* * *

As Cindy and I sat with Daddy, he gradually grew more agitated. He insisted on pulling off his oxygen. We removed it so he wouldn't do so. They gave him more morphine, which improved his agitation eventually. Cindy and I left to go eat some supper, gone but a for a little while, returning at 8:30. He continued to be restless, but would settle down completely by the time we left at 9:30.

The nurse was given the okay to give the morphine by injection. She would begin administering it under the skin, not into the muscle; she said that would be more comfortable for him. I certainly want to do whatever we can to keep him pain-free and comfortable, if that is possible. She had given him an injection at 8:10. I am not sure if she gave him the 5 ccs or the 10. (He can now have up to 10 ccs per hour, instead of every two hours.) The longer we stayed, the calmer he became, his left hand resting on the bear that Cindy and I had given him soon after his arrival in High Point 48 days ago.

His fever had broken. I am unsure of his blood pressure or heart rate, but he was still on oxygen and apparently was all right with that.

Before leaving, I tidied the room some. I got the "AA" chip that his doctor friend from Lumberton had given to him when he had visited several days ago. I also secured the stone of "FAITH" that Mama had given him that Friday; he had wanted to make sure that I had put it with his glasses that day. I know these two items, and perhaps others, will go into his pocket in the casket. I also retrieved his glasses from the chest of drawers and threw away some of the food that people had brought, putting it in the trashcan. I took his supper tray and placed it near the door to be picked up. Obviously, he had not eaten *any* of it. There would be no stories shared over a meal on this night. While I was finishing up, Carol called. I went out into the hall and talked to her; we were both crying.

The reality of Daddy's death is beginning to settle in. We had a very moving conversation, realizing that he no longer simply "has" cancer and is "going" to die. We now know that his death is imminent. I told her how hard the funeral would be, asking her to pray for me that I would be strong for Daddy. She had contacted her pastor, asking him to be ready to be a support for us, but not to do the funeral. I had received a card from him a couple of weeks ago. It was very appropriate and to the point: Daddy is dying and he is praying for us. Carol told me that he had prayed on the phone with her tonight as well.

(Before Carol called, the nurse had checked Daddy. His fever had been 101; his pulse was 132. His blood pressure was 50/?; she could not get a reading on the bottom number. She had given him a Tylenol suppository. When they turned him, she said that Daddy had grabbed her arm, like he did not want to be put on his side, so she left him on his back. It was at this time that she began the morphine injections. It dripped from his mouth when she had turned him, so it was clear that he was not getting it by the dropper method. Along with the morphine at 8:10, she had already given him an Ativan at 7:00 due to his extreme agitation. They both seemed to be helping him. By 7:45, before Cindy and I had returned, he had a smile on his face, perhaps from the Ativan? He looked quite pleasant. At that time, Cindy and I had left to eat.)

After speaking with Carol, Cindy and I went back into the room, discovering that Daddy was still restful. The TV was on low volume, the *History Channel*, and the radio was still on as well. I talked to the nurse on the way out about the funeral arrangements and the body being moved, etc. She asked about his teeth; I told her that they would go with the body. David and Lynda had brought Daddy a crucifix yesterday that has been around his neck since their arrival. The nurse told me that should Daddy die tonight, she would put it in the narcotics "lockbox," if I am not present. I told her to call me if his death was taking place, stressing, "I plan to be here." I can call for the necklace, however, *if* he dies without my being present.

Feeling settled about the potential scenario, Cindy and I left. I told her on the way home that while I don't know if this is the last time I will see Daddy here, it very well could be; we *must* be ready for that. I did not sleep well Sunday night. I was not able to relax for thinking we would get a call tonight.

CHAPTER 35

MONDAY, JANUARY 3

The Good Eye Cries

It's odd to see someone in pain and yet you've got to give them enough morphine to keep them out of pain. It's a strange contrast.

Arriving at the nursing home for breakfast around 8:15, I found Daddy alert and looking around, but not aware of whom I was, though clearly aware of my presence. He was not terribly agitated initially, but became more so as I sat with him.

The nurse had given him one-half dose of his morphine a few minutes before I arrived; he could have the other half if needed. He seemed to ease some within a few minutes, but insisted on pulling the oxygen off of his nose. I managed to feed him a little oatmeal, *very* little. (Oatmeal is the last food that he would eat before his death.) I gave him a small amount on the end of the spoon. I had asked the nurse if he would aspirate, but she said that if he would eat it, then it was probably okay. He did not choke, but ate little of it. Eventually, after three or four small teaspoons, he seemed to become unaware that I was attempting to feed him. However, I swabbed his mouth with water several times. He would move his tongue on the swab and then close his mouth around it like a sucker. I also managed to give him one full swab of coffee, appropriately enough, the last fluid that he would ever drink. Eventually, however, he became unresponsive when I placed the swab to his lips. It was obvious that even involuntary reflexes were stopping.

I decided to call Scott with an update as I had promised him last night. He suggested removing the oxygen if it was irritating Daddy. He also told me that it should be all right to do so, if Daddy appeared to be breathing fairly easy. He seemed to be breathing normally and was not taking short breaths like he had at one point last night, so I removed the oxygen. He also had the stuffed bear by his side; the one that Cindy and I had given him upon his arrival in High Point on that day that now seems so long ago…

In a few minutes, he began to move his arms again like he couldn't be still. He began to moan as if in pain. He also clenched his fists, holding the sheets with either hand. I called the nurse. She gave him the other one-half dose of his morphine. It was only 45 minutes after he had received the first one, but he was *very* restless.

Daddy's eyes are open, sort of aware, but no words are ever spoken on this day, only moans. When he settles down some, he makes constant motions with his hands. It is impossible to know what they represent or what he may be seeing during these times. It is clear that he is hurting. The morphine seems to ease it, though not completely. He soon goes into another mode of hurting again. I guess the cycle has begun. I really do not know what to do. I know the morphine represses his suffering, but also his respiration.

He has developed a cough as well, but it is non-productive. He does not have the energy to clear anything out of his throat. I do not know what to do about that. He is miserable, and I don't know how much more he is able to take. He flinches and moans. I can only imagine the agony that he is in.

I sit by his bed and silently pray, "Dear Lord, if it is possible, if it is in Your will, may he be relieved of his suffering. May today be the day that he dies."

It is agony to me. I don't want to see him die; nobody does. I won't be ready, even though I have tried to prepare myself. But I know that what breaks my heart is not that he will be gone (although that will break my heart), but even more so is to see how he suffers. I can't take that. He twitches and looks around, but with-

out apparent seeing. He moans and touches his right side, like it's hurting. I just don't know what to do for him.

They came in and said that they were going to bathe him. I know that he needs to be cleaned up, but I asked them to be gentle and keep an eye on him. We don't want to over-medicate him, but if he is in obvious pain, don't hesitate to give him up to what he can have. The nurse assured me that she would. I think that it is obvious that Death is watching, and waiting. His prize is at hand. The end is near. Daddy simply goes through phases. His pain is increasing; I think that is clear.

* * *

After eating an Italian sub from *Subway*, Daddy's favorite sandwich, Cindy and I arrived at the nursing home around 12:30. I had called Carol just before lunch. She was on her way, but was planning to eat before getting to the nursing home.

Daddy's breathing was different than it had been this morning. It was now shallow and coming in quick breaths. His eyes were fixed and slightly open; it was obvious that he was dying. I swabbed his mouth. He did not respond, nor did he swallow, that I noticed. Carol soon arrived. We both sat on the loveseat at the left side of Daddy's bed. (Scott had brought it in from the TV room on Daddy's hall during one of his previous visits when seating was at a premium.) Carol and I watched him and talked to one another softly. His breathing was becoming more and more shallow as we observed him. He was not moving. He was totally different from how I had found him this morning. Now, he looked to be at peace. He did not appear to be in any pain. As we sat there, Carol's cell phone rang; it was Ashly. She went into the hall to take the call while I got up and went to stand on Daddy's right side near the window. I held his right hand and gently rubbed his forearm and chest, speaking encouraging words to him.

He exhaled and stopped breathing for several seconds. I told Cindy to go and get Carol, telling her, "It's time." Carol came in as Daddy's breathing continued to grow more shallow. He would stop breathing for several seconds, only to catch yet another breath. He would breathe shallowly for several seconds before exhaling and not catching his breath for several more seconds. I told Carol that the time was getting "very close."

We both began to whisper to him, Carol in his left ear, and I in his right. We held his hands and rubbed his arms and chest soothingly. I whispered several things in his ear, while my head rested against his. He was sweating and clammy. His arms were becoming noticeably cold. Among the things that I told him were:

"Daddy, it's all right for you to go. We release you and let you go."

"You are in the arms of Jesus. You are in his hands. I leave you there. I pray that you don't suffer anymore. Your suffering is almost over."

"I will see you again and I will do what I can, with God's help, to make sure that the rest of your children see you again also."

"Daddy, your purpose for coming to High Point is now completed. Relax and rest."

I stepped back to look at him. His eyes fully opened, for just a couple of seconds and he looked at us. As he closed them again, his face relaxed. He squeezed them shut more tightly as a single tear flowed from his right eye, his *good* eye. With his eyes still closed, he took two short breaths and stopped breathing. He never struggled; he never rattled. He died at 2:00 today. He looked peaceful, though his mouth was open.

I feel in my heart that the tear was one of joy. As I have referenced earlier, Daddy's "good eye" did not cry, according to him. Today, however, it cried; but I do not believe that it was from sadness. It cried for joy at seeing the glorious things that were awaiting him, and us, *if* we place our trust in the sacrifice of Jesus, God's only Son. I know now that the tear of joy is the last tear he will ever cry, for now he is at that place where there is no crying and where "God will wipe away every tear from their eyes" (Revelation 21:4a, NKJV). Daddy has achieved what we all long for: eternal peace and joy.

Carol, Cindy and I were hugging and crying. The mood was more one of release, not sadness, though we were sad. We were talking to him as he died. He passed over peacefully. We could not have asked for him to go more peacefully than he did. He did not appear to be in any pain.

After 10 minutes or so, I told Cindy to go and get the nurse. (I had told Carol that we could take our time with the body and not be in a terrible hurry; we get the opportunity to be with our father at his death only once.) She and I removed his oxygen and turned off the machine. We took a few minutes with him before we sent Cindy to get the nurse. We pulled the covers up over his chest and straightened him in the bed. I combed his hair; he looked peaceful when the nurse came in. She checked him and pronounced that he was indeed dead. I called Sammy. Carol called Scott, but was unable to get an answer. She also called Lynda so she could inform David. (We thought she could tell him better than one of us on the phone.) He was probably "up to his elbows" in prescriptions, it being the first of the month. Lynda did tell David, I found out later, about 3:00. When he saw her coming into the store, he said that he knew what the news was before she ever opened her mouth. Somehow, he managed to finish work today. It was the biggest day that the store has had, up to this point, as I referenced earlier. Daddy was no doubt smiling from heaven!

Sammy seemed to take the news reasonably well. He told me that he would be in touch with the funeral home in Wallace right away. I told him that someone from the funeral home in High Point was on the way to retrieve Daddy's body.

Carol and I had been on the patio of the 100 hall making our telephone calls, when O. W. Willis, one of the three part-time chaplains who works with me, came by the window. He was making calls today and wanted to check on Daddy. He entered the room after Daddy had died, prayed with the body and left his card, noting the date and time on the back. As he left the room, he saw me on the patio. He came out and we immediately embraced. O. W. had prayed for Daddy's salvation, with tears in his eyes, a couple of times in my office. He had visited him several times and Daddy had told me on one occasion that O. W. was "one of the most interesting persons I know." They had talked about some aspect of southern Indiana's history (O. W. is from there) with which Daddy was familiar. O. W. has been a tremendous support to me. As I cried, he told me how sorry he was, but also how fulfilling it is to know that we had been able to get Daddy prepared for this time. He reminded me of God's grace in this whole situation. I told him, "Pray for me." He knew that I was thinking about the funeral to come. He prayed for me there near the door after he and I had come back into the TV room.

As he exited, I went back to Daddy's room; Carol had begun to tidy up. We both remarked that we get busy when we are in stressful situations. Cindy and I also began to help pick up the room. Carol and I talked about the body before us, that it was not really Daddy, only his "shell." I reminded her that we will see him again and that the body is simply what we have known of him. I think Carol will be okay. "Okay," however, as Daddy would say, "is a relative term."

John Vernon, the executive pastor where I serve, and Steve McEuen, the Young Adult pastor, soon came by as well. Philip Siebbeles, the pastor at our home church in Rose Hill, also came. He had driven three hours to visit Daddy, but was too late. I thanked them all, testifying to the evidence of God's grace in this situation. As we stood in the hallway, just outside of Daddy's door, we all put our arms around each other. John prayed, thanking God for His grace over the last several days and weeks. He also prayed for strength in the days ahead, especially for the funeral and the times to follow. John and Steve soon left, while Phil stayed on to help us.

Everyone had been informed. The CNA that Daddy had helped with the gas bill came into the room. She was visibly crying and told us that Daddy had impacted her life more than any resident she has ever known. She asked us if she could have a plant to remember him by, indicating a ceramic sleigh on top of the closet. I told her, "If Daddy was here and you came in and asked him if you could have that plant, you know what he would say? 'Sure!'" She left the room, wiping her eyes as she went out with her treasure.

Cindy, Carol and I continued to work on the room. Carol had earlier gone to get a tote from *Big Lots*, into which we now proceeded to put all of Daddy's belongings. Phil had left to get another one. While he was gone, we finished packing everything and put it in my car to take home. Carol and I decided to separate the items depending on who had brought them to Daddy. I would keep the cards and clothes, eventually putting everything left together, along with Daddy's wallet and checkbook. I'm not sure when I will be ready to go through the items again, but I will do so later. I plan to put the bear that we gave him, however, where it can be seen. But the other items will go into totes for "future reference," as Daddy would have said.

On the way out to our cars, we noticed the bird feeders and went to retrieve them. We added them to the rest of the items already loaded and left for our house. Mike arrived just as we were leaving. He and Carol would spend the night with us, leaving early Tuesday morning to go to Wallace. Pastor Phil also headed home.

How is it possible to pack up a person's entire life in just a few minutes? How can we neatly put all of its items away, almost as if they are suddenly insignificant? Daddy's life was made up of 77 years of struggle and hope, yet it all comes down to this? Just as he quietly slipped away, so do the things that gave his life significance. But he didn't leave insignificant belongings to us, rather a vivid picture of God's grace, a grace that he only came to fully know over the last several weeks. "God, help us to understand that all of our lives, regardless of our successes, faults or shortcomings, are significant to You. Help me, in the days ahead, to show others the significance of my father's life. Amen."

I went to Italy with Ashly and Daddy in the summer of 1996.
Here, we are posing by a fountain in Assisi,
the birthplace of St. Francis.

This picture, from the fall of 1996, was almost never taken.
Cindy and I ran into Daddy and Carol on the second floor of the
Mast Store historical site near Boone, NC, completely by accident.
We ended up spending the entire evening together.

Daddy greets Carol's poodle, "Corky," at Sammy's in the late 1990s.
It has been a family tradition to go to Sammy and Sandra's house
at Christmas for years.

Sammy and Sandra lost their home to Hurricane Floyd in 1999. This picture of Daddy, Sammy, Austin (and their dog "Beaver") and David was taken Christmas at the house they were renting that year.

David and Daddy were invited to Marsha's house
for a Christmas gathering in the mid '90s.
She worked at the drugstore during that time.

I don't know why, but this White Lake picture
from the mid 1990s is among my favorites.

2001 at Carol's house, in her den

Daddy leaves Carol's in 2001. This picture is another one of my
favorites. "See you soon."

All of Daddy's children at Ashly's wedding, May, 2002,
from left to right: David, Scott, Carol, me and Sammy

Daddy and Carol share a moment at Ashly's wedding.
This is the last photograph that I have of my father.

CHAPTER 36

TUESDAY, JANUARY 4

A Life in Pictures

After seeing Carol and Mike off and taking our cat, Princess, to be boarded, Cindy and I went by our church to get the sheet music that she would use for the funeral. She will be playing and singing. Finally, after 2:00, we were on the road. We went to stay with her parents in Rose Hill. We got there, but they were not home. We got Odie, our dog, settled and went to Sammy's to join the family for supper. Sammy, Sandra, Vada, Austin, Mama, Ronald, Carol, Mike, Cindy and I, David, Lynda and Pee Wee and Peggy Hill (from our home church, *Bethel Wesleyan*) were all there. The Hill's had brought some food to Sammy's. We also had a tray of cheese and cold cuts that Pastor Phil had brought earlier. Pee Wee and Peggy have been friends with the family for years. She brought corn and large "ford hook" butterbeans. Rod Hanchey, Sandra's cousin, also came by to express his condolences. He lives across the road from Sammy and Sandra. His father, Rodney, was Sandra's uncle and the son of "Cousin Dolly." Rodney passed away several years ago.

After the company left and the meal was eaten, we began to look through some pictures that Sammy and Sandra have. They are of every conceivable person in the family and cover a lot of years. We also had all of the pictures that were in Daddy's room at the nursing home. We had put them in a bag at my house, along with the items that would be with the body in the casket. The funeral home, *Padgett's* in Wallace, had told Sammy to secure 16 to 20 pictures to be used for a DVD honoring Daddy's life. It will be shown at the visitation tomorrow night. I feel sure that we will be able to order copies. We did a lot of laughing and looked at pictures for a long time tonight. While the ones for the DVD were not selected while I was there, we had narrowed it down to several that we wanted to include. Cindy and I offered the one made when I received my Doctor of Ministry (D. Min.) degree from Drew University in Madison, New Jersey in 1995. It has been in my office ever since. It includes Mama, Sammy, Carol, Cindy, Edna Hatcher (J. W. Lanier's sister, Cindy's aunt) and Daddy, as well as me, of course. Daddy has a big smile on his face and is holding the envelope that contains the degree that hangs even now on my office wall. His support and encouragement were very meaningful to me as I worked on the degree for just over two years. It is one of my favorite pictures of him. The graduation trip was a lot of fun for all who took part in it. Even as tonight, it was one of those occasions where we all thoroughly enjoyed being together.

Cindy and I left for her parents' house around 9:30. We are to be at the funeral home in Wallace for the first viewing tomorrow morning at 10:00. *It may be hard.*

CHAPTER 37

WEDNESDAY, JANUARY 5

Sharing Stories

When Cindy and I arrived at the funeral home this morning, Sammy came out to greet us; Carol was already there. Mike, Scott and Kelly would soon arrive. (Scott and Kelly spent last night with Mike and Carol.) Vada and Austin soon came with Sandra also. David and Lynda were not able to make the first viewing.

As Sammy, Cindy, Carol and I walked in, we proceeded to the small room on the left. Rather than waiting for the funeral home personnel to slide back the accordion door, Carol and I went on in. Sammy said that we might need to wait; we told him that it was our daddy, and I already knew the probable procedure. In a moment, after we had gone into the room where the body was, the funeral director came by. He asked us how the body looked. We were generally pleased. A dead body can only look so good (to me), but I must admit that they did do a nice job.

Daddy was dressed in the dark suit that he had worn to Ashly's wedding. He also had on the dark blue shirt and bright tie used for that happy occasion. He looked very restful. His color was not that good, but he still looked as if he was simply asleep.

Daddy had cracked a nail on one of his fingers as a boy. His finger was run over by a wagon of some sort on a bridge. That nail always grew with a crack in it. Sammy repositioned Daddy's hands so that the finger with the cracked nail was visible. I'm not sure if

anyone would notice it, but it was not visible before Sammy repositioned his hands.

Carol had brought the items that we wanted to put with the
body. We put his glasses on him, but did not feel that it looked natural. We decided to put them in the left, outside pocket of the jacket.
They were poking out ever so slightly, as if he might take them out
to use them at any moment.

In his right inside breast pocket, I placed the following items.
They, and the glasses, would remain with him through the burial
and not be removed:

*He had the "stone of FAITH" that Mama gave him that Friday
(the one that he was clutching in his right hand; he had told me to
put it in the drawer with his glasses that day).*

*He had a fork from our kitchen. Daddy may have even used it
when he came to visit us over a year ago. Cindy had cooked pork
ribs. He had eaten seconds, along with other items that she had
prepared. The fork, however, was symbolic of desert, a theme I
would explain at the funeral in my closing illustration. Daddy
wanted the illustration to be used. He often said the words, "Don't
forget the fork."*

*He had the one-year anniversary blue "AA" chip given to him
by the doctor from Lumberton when he had visited.*

*He had a copy, no, the same actual copy of the article on John
Wesley that I read to him while he was in the hospital in High Point.
He had asked about Wesley's last words. He had actually visited
Wesley's gravesite in England. Wesley's words would become one
of Daddy's favorite quotes and the words that he wanted on his
headstone: "But the best of all is, God is with us."*

I also put the teddy bear that Cindy and I had gotten at the mall
in High Point the day that he came to be with us at the nursing
home. I rested it on his left side, looking out, almost as if he was
providing comfort for him. The bear was at Daddy's left side the
day that he died; it is on his left side now. I plan to keep it after the
visitation is over tonight. It will forever be a precious reminder of
him. His hand was on it several times during the last two days of his

life. Carol said that she would encourage him to rub it instead of the covers during those times when his hands were reaching out for something to provide comfort.

David plans to drape the crucifix Daddy wore over his hands as well, removing it after the visitation tonight. He and Lynda gave it to Daddy the last time they were in High Point just a few days ago. It was around his neck when he took his final breath. I removed it and put it around my neck when Carol and I were cleaning out his room; it was one of the first things I did after he died in order to make sure that it was safe. I have not taken it off since then, but will give it to David this evening to put with Daddy. I am sure it will be a very meaningful reminder to him of Daddy; he might even choose to wear it himself.

We did not shed many tears during this first visitation, but I cried this morning while I was walking Odie. I told him that we would need to walk a little longer than usual…

Daddy looks much more at peace than he did Monday morning when he was in such agony. I am sure, nevertheless, that I will shed many more tears for him in the days ahead.

We shared some stories as we sat in the room with the body. All those who would be there for this visitation had arrived. Sammy told a story about an incident in Rose Hill at the drug store; it occurred when he was young. A man had asked for something for his stomach, so Sammy gave him an Alka-Seltzer. When he turned around to get the water for the man, he had already taken them without anything to drink. The man was quickly uncomfortable, so Sammy asked Daddy what to do and he told him to get the man some water. We all laughed; Sammy laughed as well, even though he was numb on the left side of his face. He had to have a root canal done earlier today because he has a tooth that bothered him last night. It was one of those unavoidable things.

He told another story about a woman who came into the store pulling at her hair and wringing her hands, obviously emotionally distressed. Daddy told him to take her through the back door of the store to Dr. Hawes. Dr. Hawes delivered several of us children into this world, including me. He and Daddy were long-time friends. He had an office in a building not far from the back of the drug store in

Rose Hill. On the way, the woman grabbed Sammy, struggling, but he eventually got her to the doctor. We all laughed about the situation as he told it to us.

In a bit, everyone seemed satisfied to leave. On the way out, I picked up a calendar from the desk near the door. I plan to keep it with the other items that I will keep of my father's. Cindy and I went home to her parents' house, and I worked on Daddy's funeral. We plan to go back for the visitation this evening. It will be from 7:00-9:00.

* * *

Back at Sadie and J. W.'s house, Pastor Aron called. I was working on the funeral at the time. He told me he regretted that he could not make it to the funeral, but wanted to let me know he was praying for me and that I was in his thoughts. As I stood in their kitchen and talked to him, I told him that I appreciate his support and the support of the church. I reminded him of what he told me during a prayer time that the staff had not long after I came to serve at *High Point First*. He told me then that, "God not only redeems prodigal sons, but he can redeem prodigal fathers as well." At that time, he and the staff laid hands on my shoulders and offered prayer for Daddy. I never forgot his statement, however. How prophetic it proved to be. God has surely answered that prayer. Before our phone conversation ended, he prayed with me yet again, asking God for strength during the funeral and in the days ahead.

* * *

Cindy and I took the short drive to Sammy's for the meal before tonight's visitation, arriving at 5:00. Cindy and I, Scott, Kelly, Mike, Carol, Sammy, Sandra, Vada, Austin, Mama, Ronald, David and Lynda were all there; we ate supper together. Northeast Pentecostal Free-Will Baptist Church, near Sammy's house, provided the food. Mac Raynor and a couple of other ladies were just leaving after bringing the food. They brought lots of food and several deserts, creating an impressive spread. We left at 6:30 in separate cars, planning to arrive at the funeral home by 6:45. We all were there on time, with David and Lynda arriving a few minutes later. Daddy's visitation was in the chapel of *Padgett's*.

The casket was open and placed in the very center at the front of the chapel. Daddy's body was just as we had last seen it, the bear still with him. On either side of the casket, and behind it on the platform, were flowers from lots of people; some of the names I recognized, others I did not. (We had requested that in lieu of flowers, donations in Daddy's memory should be made to either *Hospice* or the *American Cancer Society*.) Several feet from the head, on the left side of the chapel, was a large television playing the DVD for which we had submitted the pictures. On the top was the DVD case, complete with Daddy's picture (the one from Greece, on the boat) along with his name. The same picture was also used on the front of the programs put together by the funeral home. The picture is one of my favorites, although it was taken a world away. Daddy looks very content, has a scarf around his neck, a smile on his face, and the wind blowing in his hair. I will forever remember that picture when I think of him.

The DVD was very moving. As if our emotions were not unsettled enough, we all watched it and cried openly, mesmerized. It presented several pictures, including the one from Greece, the one from Drew University, some from Ashly's wedding and a very early one of Daddy and Mama. The music was an orchestral arrangement without any vocals. I know that the pain will eventually ease, while the wonderful memories will stay, but tonight will be the last time I want to watch the DVD for many days. While I plan to order a copy, I probably will put it away until I feel like I am ready to look at it again.

The music sounded like an old Irish tune, one that I did not know. Carol commented to Scott and me that it had words like "Beat the drum slowly and play the fife lowly." Scott and I were dumbfounded. While I did not record Daddy's comments about a song he mentioned in the dining room at the nursing home on Monday, December 27 (exactly one week before his death), Daddy had asked Scott and I if we knew the song that had the words, "Beat the drum slowly and play the fife lowly?" I had told him on that day that I wasn't familiar with it. Needless to say, Carol's comments made me very interested in finding out more about it. Scott and I were floored that out of thousands of songs available, the funeral home would pick the very one that Daddy referenced that we did not know. (We asked the funeral home director; the song was literally chosen at random.)

* * *

I investigated the song on the Internet later, discovering that it is indeed an Irish tune that has been used to create at least 12 versions of the song. The theme is always the same, i.e. someone has been mortally wounded and is dying, though the character in the song is sometimes a woman, sometimes a man. Daddy was probably referencing the American version called *A Cowboy's Lament* or *The Streets of Laredo*. It is a morbid and sobering song. The tune is simple, yet beautiful. I now know something about it and plan to secure an audio copy in the near future. Burl Ives has recorded it, among others. The words to *A Cowboy's Lament* are:

As I walked out in the streets of Laredo
As I walked out in Laredo one day
I spied a young cowboy wrapped up in white linen
Wrapped up in white linen and cold as the clay.

"I see by your outfit that you are a cowboy"
These words he did say as I boldly stepped by
"Come sit down beside me and hear my sad story
I'm shot in the breast and I know I must die."

"Oh beat the drum slowly and play the fife lowly
Play the Dead March as you carry me along
Take me to the green valley and lay the sod o'er me
For I'm a young cowboy and I know I've done wrong."

"It was once in the saddle I used to go dashing
It was once in the saddle I used to go gay
First to the dram house and then to the card house
Got shot in the breast and I'm dying today."

"Get six jolly cowboys to carry my coffin
Get six pretty maidens to bear up my pall
Put branches of roses all over my coffin
Put roses to deaden the clods as they fall."

"Go bring me a cup, a cup of cold water
To cool my parched lips," the young cowboy said
Before I returned, the spirit had left him
And gone to its Maker, the cowboy was dead.

We beat the drum slowly and played the fife lowly
And bitterly wept as we bore him along
For we all loved our comrade, so brave, young and handsome
We all loved our comrade, although he'd done wrong.

* * *

The DVD is very tastefully done from the cover to the content. It runs for just over five minutes, the pictures interspersed with video of nature scenes.

People started filing into the chapel. Some of them I didn't know, but many of them were friends. There were a few from High Point, including Myra Snider, my former secretary who still does volunteer work with the seniors. She visited Daddy both at the nursing home and the hospital in High Point. David Keith and his wife Wanda also came. David is one of the three part-time chaplains who serve with me in the Senior Adult ministries of our church. John Vernon and his wife Kim were also there. John had come by the nursing home on the day that Daddy died. I was glad to see them all, especially Myra. She has become a good friend and comrade in ministry; she is a very special person.

People came steadily until approximately 8:40. So many were there: people from *Bethel Wesleyan Church*, Lumberton, people who were in high school with Daddy and people from Wallace and Rose Hill. Gene Pierce and his wife were there. He worked with Daddy years ago at the drug store in Rose Hill. His wife was over-joyed that Daddy had come to the Lord. She said, "Sam was the most brilliant person I have ever known." Everyone was so kind. I did not cry during the visitation itself, but cried quite a bit watching the DVD before people had started coming into the chapel.

By 9:30 Cindy and I, along with Mike, Carol, Scott and Kelly, left. We were literally the last ones to leave. Before we left, however, I got the bear out of the casket. David had also removed the crucifix, which he had draped over Daddy's hands during the visitation. On the way out the envelope containing the pictures was given to us. It had been on the desk near the main entrance. Each picture had a sticker on the back with the number of the order in which it appears on the DVD. I took the Drew picture out of the envelope and commented to Carol that I would like a copy of the picture taken at her house of Daddy and me. She told me that I could have it. She also said that she had the frames for both in her car. The six of us walked out together to her car. She had the frames in a bag. I put the two frames in our car, along with both pictures, and left the funeral home. The Drew picture will go back in my office, while the one from Carol's house will go to our home.

I had several people tonight to say that they "could not do the funeral," or they asked, "How will you get through it?" My response was always the same: On the day after Daddy found out that he had cancer, Sammy and I had asked him about his funeral arrangements. Daddy had asked us "What do we need to talk about?" that day, clearly providing an opening to discuss his funeral. When I asked him about who should do it, he had said, "You are really the only minister that I have, I want you to do it." At that time, I was optimistic, even honored (I still am.) But, as the reality of it sets in, I am beginning to get a little nervous about it. However, it is the last thing that I can do that my father specifically requested of me. "I am praying for 45 minutes of grace" tomorrow, for Cindy, my family and myself. God's grace has been so evident throughout my father's illness and death; I am convinced that it will be sufficient for the funeral and beyond. That is the answer that I gave to those who asked me.

"Lord, make it so."

CHAPTER 38

THURSDAY, JANUARY 6

I Have Never Felt Like I Do Today

Today, we are going to bury our Daddy.

This morning, I got up and walked Odie. It was overcast and milder than usual. It was already in the upper 50s early. It was going to be a balmy day for the time of year. As I walked I prayed, asking God for grace for the family. I asked for God's grace for Cindy as she plays the piano and then sings. I asked for God's grace for Pastor Phil as he assists me with the funeral. And I asked for God's grace for myself to help me get through this. Breaking the news to David about Daddy's cancer was *one* of the most difficult things that I have ever done. But this is, by far, the hardest thing that I have ever attempted to do. I want to do the best that I can and say what needs to be said. I want to be able to do it without being terribly upset. *"God, your grace was sufficient for my Daddy, and it is sufficient for us as we go through the service to remember him and the tremendous gift that you have given our father, as well as all of us."*

* * *

Cindy and I arrived at *Bethel Wesleyan Church* around 10:25 a. m. The funeral service itself would be at 11:00. She soon went in and began playing as people arrived. In the parking lot I spoke with Dan Price and Myra Snider. Dan had driven down just this morning from

High Point to attend the funeral. Dan and his wife, Naomi, are very active in our church. Cindy and I are members of the small group that meets in their home each week. Also, I am the pastoral representative for our church on the Wesleyan Arms Board, of which Dan is a member. The nursing home, the one where Daddy lived, is an affiliate of our church. Dan and Naomi both are heavily involved in the senior adult ministry of our church.

I also greeted the pallbearers near the door. They were just getting ready to go into the church; the body was already there. They included Delwood Raynor, my brother by my mother's second husband; Gary Wells, son of my father's sister, Sissie; (I did Gary's dad's funeral about two years ago in Wallace.) Andy Cavenaugh, my father's brother R. C.'s son; Jason Henderson, Carol and Mike's son; Eric Davis, Carol's son by her first marriage; and Austin Cavanaugh, Sammy's son. I also spoke to Gary's brother, Stewart, and his wife. He and Gary know what it is to lose a father. Andy's father also died about two years ago. I assisted with his funeral as well.

I went into the narthex of the church and picked up a bulletin that the church had provided. Pastor Phil and I had worked on getting it put together, and it included an order of service, the words to *Amazing Grace* and a personal message of thanks to everyone for their prayers and support during the passing of our father.

I stood with Frank Murray by the door that leads into the sanctuary. He is from the church and was helping hand out bulletins and providing general assistance to those who were attending the funeral. He and I greeted various people as they came in; we also talked with each other.

Speaking with the people was not too difficult. But I began to cry openly when I saw other people from High Point arrive. All of those who were at the visitation were there today as well. But a group also came on our senior adult bus, *The Silver Treads*, from our church in High Point. When I saw them getting off the bus, I was overwhelmed by the show of support. Those who rode the bus included Debbie Barwick, our office administrator; Carla Meadows, my secretary; Cher Limpach, director of our small group ministry and my former secretary; Inthava Inthisane, pastor to our

Laotian congregation; John Butt, volunteer bus driver; and Melvin Howard, who helps me with the various facility worship services on a rotating schedule, both singing and preaching. His wife died in Greensboro after several months in the hospital not long ago. He is very well acquainted with grief.

Others came separately, including Reitzell and Peggy Nance who drove from High Point just this morning; they help us with hospital visitation. Dan LeRoy, our district superintendent, and James Smith, who works with David Keith and O. W. Willis as a part-time chaplain, rode together. James first told Aron Willis about my potential availability for the position in which I now serve. Also, four of our pastors, including John Vernon, came down; I could see them through the entrance window. They included Steve McEuen, who came with John to the nursing home the day that Daddy died; Rob MacCallum, pastor to children and teens; and Jonathan Lewis, pastor to middle adults and missions pastor. All but John rode together in Jonathan's car. I was okay with Steve and Rob, but cried as I hugged Jonathan. He and I both attended Southern Wesleyan University in the mid 1980s, though he was one year behind me. He and I, along with two other guys, traveled to nine youth camps in 1985 as representatives of the school. He lost his father to cancer several years ago after a lengthy battle. He has told me that they were best friends. His father was suffering about the same time of year as Daddy, dying in December. I cried because I know that Jonathan can identify with my situation very closely. It really means a lot to me that he came to the funeral.

Just before 11:00, the family arrived. I stepped outside and spoke to several of them. As Cindy continued to play, I led the family into the sanctuary. I took my place on the platform near Phil who was already there. We asked the congregation to be seated and the service began. The order of service was as follows:

Musical Prelude

Seating of the Family

Opening Scripture

Special Music

Scripture/Prayer

Special Music

Message

Special Music

Prayer of Benediction

Musical Postlude

God gave me strength to get through the service. I did struggle at times, even once feeling that I would not get through it, but was able to do so. Cindy also did a good job, both with her playing, as well as her singing. I cried when she began to sing.

For the opening scripture I read 2 Corinthians 4:7-5:9 from the New Living Translation (NLT). It is the scripture that includes the reference that Sammy had written in the card he sent Daddy while he was in the hospital in High Point. I had read this passage to Daddy while he was in the hospital and at least once in the nursing home, perhaps twice. The part that speaks about short suffering was especially meaningful. 4:17 reads, "For our present troubles are quite small and won't last very long. Yet they produce for us an immeasurably great glory that will last forever!" (NLT). How very appropriate for our present situation. The song by Josh Groban was next. The music has an Irish flavor and is a very beautiful reminder of God's provision. Ashly provided the CD. The words to *You Raise Me Up* are:

When I am down and, oh my soul, so weary
When troubles come and my heart burdened be
Then, I am still and wait here in the silence
Until you come and sit a while with me

You raise me up, so I can stand on mountains
You raise me up, to walk on stormy seas
I am strong, when I am on your shoulders
You raise me up...to more than I can be

(The second verse, or chorus, was repeated three more times and ended with the tag line, "You raise me up...to more than I can be".)

The song is one that Cindy and I both fell in love with several weeks ago. To hear it at Daddy's funeral was very meaningful indeed. Carol had requested it.

As I heard the song again today, the words, almost as a sooth-ing balm, spoke to my heart but reminded me once more of Daddy's suffering. He certainly knew what it was to be weary and have a burdened heart, though I trust that his burden was lifted to some extent during his time with us. But as I think back on it, I wonder how many times he waited in the silence of his room at the nursing home for me or the others to come and "sit a while" with him. I hope that our presence lifted him up. And today, I know that he is soaring above the mountains of suffering and the seas of illness...At this time, he has indeed reached a higher place than any on this earth. God's grace is so real.

After reading Scripture, Phil led us in prayer; Cindy then sang. The song is based on two passages of scripture, Isaiah 40:31:

But those who hope in the LORD will renew their strength. They will soar on wings like eagles; they will run and not grow weary, they will walk and not be faint.

And Psalm 91:1-4, 9-12:

He who dwells in the shelter of the Most High will rest in the shadow of the Almighty. I will say of the LORD, "He is my refuge and my fortress, my God, in whom I trust." Surely he will save you from the fowler's snare and from the deadly pestilence. He will cover you with his feathers, and under his wings you will find refuge; his faithfulness will be your shield and to guard you in all your ways; they will lift you up in their hands, so that you will not strike your foot against a stone.

The words to *On Eagle's Wings* are:

> *You who dwell in the shelter of the Lord*
> *Who abide in His Shadow for life*
> *Say to the Lord: "My refuge,*
> *My rock in whom I trust!"*
>
> *And He will raise you up on eagle's wings*
> *Bear you on the breath of dawn*
> *Make you to shine like the sun*
> *And hold you in the palm of his hand*
>
> *The snare of the fowler will never capture you*
> *And famine will bring you no fear*
> *Under his wings your refuge*
> *His faithfulness your shield*
>
> *And He will raise you up on eagle's wings*
> *Bear you on the breath of dawn*
> *Make you to shine like the sun*
> *And hold you in the palm of his hand*
>
> *For to His angels He's given a command*
> *To guard you in all of your ways*
> *Upon their hands they will bear you up*
> *Let you dash your foot against the stone*

And He will raise you up on eagle's wings
Bear you on the breath of dawn
Make you to shine like the sun
And hold you in the palm of his hand

And hold you; hold you in the palm of his hand

After she finished, I got up to share the message. I read Ephesians 2:1-10. My outline was as follows, though I went into considerably more detail:

INTRODUCTION:
Thank *everyone* for all they have done and for their presence today.

Thank *my family* for their help and support for Daddy over these last eight weeks or so.

Most of all, I want to *thank God* and our Lord Jesus Christ, for giving Daddy the opportunity to prepare himself spiritually.

I THANK GOD FOR HIS GRACE…His grace was extended to Daddy, and us, in several ways:

Daddy had the grace of a supportive family.
Daddy had the grace to touch others.
—I shared the story about he CNA that Daddy assisted with the gas bill, and read from two of his get-well cards.
Daddy had the grace of time.
Daddy had the grace of salvation.
—I shared that Daddy never complained (literally).
—I told the story about his "good eye" and "bad eye" and the significance of his "good eye" crying a single tear when he died.
—I also told the story of how Carol and I were blessed to have been with him at the very end.

I concluded my remarks with the story of the fork. I informed them that Daddy has a fork in his pocket even now. I read the story, *You Can Keep the Fork*, which Daddy had referenced to me early on. I know someone had passed it on to him and he loved the story.

I also know that it meant a lot to him, so I shared it at his funeral. While I actually read the story, I summarize it here:

An elderly lady found out that she had cancer. She called in her pastor, telling him that she had some items relative to her funeral that she wanted to share with him. She gave him the songs that she wanted included. She gave him the scripture that she wanted read. And she told him that she wanted her Bible in one hand and a fork in the other. He said that he understood about the Bible, but didn't understand the fork. She then told him that the fork represented "The best is yet to come." At church dinners, she explained, when they took away the dishes, they would say to "Keep your fork." That meant that desert was coming, not Jell-O, or pudding, or even ice cream. It meant the good stuff, like chocolate cake or cherry pie. She knew that the best was yet to come. She told him that she wants them to see the fork and realize that "The best is yet to come."

Daddy loved that illustration. I find comfort in knowing that he had a fork in his pocket and everyone knew that he did…and why it is there, even today.

I then told those gathered that there was no greater tribute to God's grace for my father, than to sing the words printed in the bulletin, the words to *Amazing Grace*. Although we had discussed *Blessed Assurance* as the song for his funeral so many weeks ago when he was in the hospital, God's grace had to be the obvious theme for the congregational song. I led them as we sang these words:

Amazing Grace, how sweet the sound!
That saved a wretch like me!
I once was lost, but now am found;
Was blind, but know I see.

'Twas grace that taught my heart to fear,
And grace my fears relieved.
How precious did that grace appear,
The hour I first believed.

Thro' many dangers, toils and snares
I have already come.
'Tis grace hath brought me safe thus far,
And grace will lead me home.

When we've been there ten thousand years,
Bright shining as the sun,
We've no less days to sing God's praise
Than when we first begun.

As I have already written, Daddy's funeral, without a doubt, is the hardest thing that I have done up to this point in my life. But, just as God's grace was there when we needed it most, I found it was present with me as well today. I will never use the illustration about the fork in another funeral. Out of love and honor to Daddy's memory, I have used it for the last time.

After the final song, I had the closing prayer, and then preceded the body to the hearse to begin what would be my father's last earthly journey.

* * *

Phil rode with Cindy and me to the cemetery; it is about 10 minutes from the church. Daddy was buried at Cavenaugh's Cemetery on Highway 41 East, Wallace. The cemetery has other families represented there as well. Families of those buried there keep it up; I guess we now become contributors.

Daddy's grave is located next to Uncle Frank, his brother, at the back corner of the cemetery. Other family members are buried nearby. Phil and I took our places and I read Revelation 21:1-7 from the New King James Version. I then spoke the following committal as I rested my right hand on the head of the casket. I actually rubbed the casket with my hand as I read the words:

"And now we commit this body to its resting place; and we commit the spirit of our father, grandfather, brother and friend, Sam Cavanaugh, together with every sacred interest of our hearts, into

God's keeping; praying that He will deal graciously and mercifully with each of us, until we too shall come to Him in glory, through the riches of grace in Jesus our Lord."

I was all right until the saying of Daddy's name. I had to pause and gather myself before I could say it and complete the committal. After I finished, Phil had prayer with us all. I then gave the following benediction:

"Now may the God of peace, that brought again from the dead our Lord Jesus, that Great Shepherd of the sheep, comfort and protect you now and always, through the blood of the everlasting covenant, through Jesus Our Lord; to whom be glory for ever and ever. Amen."

At that time, Phil extended an invitation to the out of town guests to join the church family at the fellowship hall for lunch. We then began to greet the family. They were seated on two rows of folding chairs, very near the coffin, under the tent. I went first, hugging and crying with them in the order in which they sat: Scott, Kelly, David, Lynda, Sammy, Sandra, Mike and Carol comprised the front row. When I got to Mike and Carol, each of them whispered to me, in turn, "Who will comfort you?" I replied, "I have Cindy and a lot of people in High Point, some of whom are here today."

I greeted the second row, including: Cindy, Vada, Austin, Ashly, Donna (Aunt Ruby's daughter), Aunt Ruby and Aunt Sissie.

We hung around for a while, and I was able to introduce Mama to several of the people from High Point. I also greeted all of the ushers, putting the carnation from my lapel on the casket spray as I walked by. The crowd was beginning to intermingle by that time, and I noticed several people were looking near the casket. I went over to see what was going on and noticed that on the cover of the vault, along with Daddy's name and the appropriate dates, was an engraving of the universal seal for pharmacy. At that time, we thought that *Mutual Drug Company* had paid for it; it was their gift to Daddy and the family. Daddy was with them for a long time, being licensed for over 50 years. It was beautiful and a very nice touch, I might add. We could not confirm, at that time, if they had indeed done it or not.

Eventually, the crowd began to disperse. Some of us had parked closer to the highway and had to walk the length of the cemetery to get to our cars. On the way several of us looked at the headstones of other family members, including Granddaddy Roland and Grandma Vada, Daddy's parents. He died in the late 1960s, she in the early 1980s. I remember him some, going to the local store, Graham Hanchey's, as a child to get a bag of candy. Granddaddy would stand me on the counter since I was so small. I remember Grandma very well. Aunt Sissie's daughter, Connie, and I would go stay the entire summer with Grandma. The home place is almost within sight of the cemetery, on the opposite side of the highway. I remember as a young teen, and even earlier, playing under the grapevines, eating cabbage kraut out of a crock in the "crib," sleeping the entire night on the front porch on a "cot," feeding cats in the smokehouse and waking up to the smell of sausage or country ham with all of the trimmings. Grandma also made biscuits that she would keep in the "safe" along with other leftovers. We would poke a hole in a cold biscuit and fill it with molasses or "Karo Syrup." Daddy and I had talked about doing that very thing a couple of days ago. He went to the same safe and did the very same thing with Grandma's biscuits that Connie and I did as children. *The best things in life never change*. I can taste that biscuit now…

As we continued to walk, Andy, the unofficial family historian, talked about why some of the family spell our name C-a-v-a-n-a-u-g-h (Daddy and his older brother Charles did), while the rest spell it C-a-v-e-n-a-u-g-h. Even the headstones testify to the discrepancy. Andy told us that he understood a teacher in grade school had told some of the family that the spelling with an "a" was accurate, while the spelling with an "e" was not correct. Daddy's joke about the rest of the family not knowing how to spell may contain more than a grain of truth. The final say as to the accuracy of Andy's explanation, however, was forever buried with Daddy today. It will continue to be a lively point of discussion for years to come, I suppose. Now, of course, we will never know the answer for certain.

* * *

We went back to the church fellowship hall for lunch. The ladies of the church had set forth a very impressive spread. We had everything from fried chicken to dessert. Everyone from High Point stayed, with the exception of John and Kim Vernon. The place was full. The fellowship hall, a white, frame building, is actually the old church and sits near the "new" church that was built in the 1970s. It is composed of one large room, which used to be the "sanctuary," with two small rooms near the front of the building. One of the rooms is a very small kitchen. The congregation has debated for years about what to do with the building, as its usefulness wanes. Today, though, it is filled with people who all thought something of our daddy in one way or another.

I sat to the left of Cindy while Austin was on my left. Across from us were Tera, Scott's sister by his mother's previous marriage, Tera's daughter Casey, Scott, Kelly, Sammy, Tim, Jeannie's husband and Jeannie Williams, who is Uncle R. C.'s daughter and Andy's sister. Uncle R. C. was Daddy's older brother. Jeannie told us that she had made a fruitcake like "Grandma Vada used to make each Christmas." She had brought what was left of it to the dinner. Grandma made fruit-cakes that were neither refrigerated nor frozen. She would put them in a cheese box wrapped in linen and placed under the bed or some other dark place. On a regular basis she would take them out, pour wine over them, wrap them up again and put them back where they had been. They were very good. The family always looked forward to them each Christmas. I would like to try and make one myself. Jeannie's was very good and reminded me that I cannot remember the last time I had a piece of "Grandma's fruitcake."

Mama, Ronald, Aunt Sissie and Connie were nearby as well. It is obvious that Daddy was both loved and respected.

Other than me, Aunt Ruby, Donna, Ashly, Carol, Mike and Scott were among the last to leave. (Cindy had gone home with her parents a bit earlier.) We stood around and talked for a good while before leaving. As many of Daddy's children as can plan to go to Sammy's a little later to eat supper and go see the grave. Having finished eating, we went to our cars and left.

* * *

As I record this on my personal recorder, I am riding around Rose Hill, going down East Railroad St. I left the fellowship hall and began recording the last several paragraphs on my recorder. I needed to get away by myself so I could make sure to get it all down. I am crossing Main St. on the corner where the fire department is located. I cross Main St. I am getting closer to the shopping center where Daddy's drug store was, the one I remember most of all as a child. It was beside Harry Rouse's grocery store. He and Daddy decided to build the small shopping center together; they were good friends. I am in front of the drug store now; it looks so small. Everything looks bigger when you are a child. I can see the plate on the bar on the inside of the front door that still says "Sam's Drug Store" from that side. The store looks much like it did when I was a young child, only more dilapidated now. The memories I have of this place could almost fill a book themselves, though my time here was fairly brief and I was of a young age. Where do the years go? To where does the time escape? It makes me sad to think that this part of our lives is gone forever. I've been by here 500 times since I left Rose Hill as a small boy, almost 31 years ago, but I have never felt like I do today.

* * *

At 4:00 Cindy and I left her parents and went back to Sammy's. His family members were the only ones present when we arrived. In a few minutes, however, Carol and Scott arrived together. They had already been by the grave, Carol told us. We mulled around for a while and finally went to the cemetery. Julie, Andy's daughter who was visiting Vada, also went with us. Vada is named after Daddy's mother; Julie is named after Daddy's grandmother. Sammy and Sandra rode with Cindy and me; I drove our car.

After parking nearby, we walked to Daddy's grave. It was covered with flowers, and flowers surrounded it as well. We talked about how we might keep flowers on it. Carol is determined to do so.

We discussed Daddy's potential headstone. It would be nice to have the pharmacy symbol, similar to the one on the vault cover, on it. Even better, have a headstone in the shape of the pharmacy symbol. We want to include John Wesley's quote, the one that Daddy became so fond of quoting himself: "But the best of all is, God is with us." I told Sammy to be sure that I get the accurate quote to him before the stone is actually prepared; I don't want to get it wrong.

Of the many cut flower arrangements, we picked two to take back to the church for placement in Daddy's memory this Sunday. (Sammy, Sandra, Cindy and I went by the church after we left the cemetery. We placed one plant on the left as you go into the narthex and another between the communion table and the podium on a small stand. Sammy got the water and I watered them both. We also went by the store at "Charity Crossroads," near the church, to get a loaf of bread for sandwiches tonight.)

We looked at several other graves, commenting on the ones that were family or held some special significance. We talked about the upkeep of the cemetery. Sammy told us that donations are what were used to keep it up. We should probably make a donation each year, he suggested. We also talked about perhaps donating enough money to put a fence around the back of the cemetery since one is needed. The cars come fairly close to some of the graves as they make the turn near where Daddy is buried. His is the last plot on that row, beside Uncle Frank's grave. Uncle R. C. is one row over in the same corner.

I remarked to Carol that I cannot remember the last time I was able to see Daddy on Father's Day; I have been away from home for so many of them. But I now know that, if possible, I will come home every Father's Day and visit Daddy's grave. We talked some more; it was a very pleasant and beautiful evening. Eventually, we all headed back to Sammy's. We would get there after our stops at the church and the store.

Back at the house, Sandra warmed up what was left over of the food that had been brought by Northeast church earlier. I joked with her as I ate some cabbage and discovered it to be ice-cold. Sandra also made coffee, and we included sandwiches in the mix. I will never drink coffee again without thinking of Daddy. He liked it with one sugar and no cream.

We talked as we ate, as well as a good while after the meal was over. Mike, Ashly, and Kelly soon arrived. We played the DVD of Daddy again, trying to come up with the words to the song, but to no avail. I told Carol that I was afraid to watch the DVD after seeing it at the funeral home. But now that I have seen it again, I am not afraid to look at it. We plan to order four additional copies to be included with the final funeral expenses. One copy comes with the package already; more are available for $20 each.

Sandra gave each of us various materials that the funeral home had provided. We each have a copy of the funeral home program with Daddy's picture on the front; it is laminated and made into a bookmark. I'm not sure if I will ever use it for pleasure reading, but a bookmark certainly would have made Daddy happy; he was a lover of books for sure. We also received a laminated copy of the obituary.

Eventually, several of us settled down to watch some TV; oddly enough, we gravitated towards the *History Channel*. I will never watch that network again without thinking of Daddy I am sure; it was one of his favorite channels. The TV in his room was on the channel the moment that he died.

All of the live plants from the funeral were there at Sammy and Sandra's house as well. She wanted to get rid of them and said that each of us should take two or three home with us; so we all took a couple. Cindy and I chose a mum, which we would give to her mother, and a large peace lily. Cindy said that it would look good on our front porch this summer. That seems so far away. I had already taken a small peace lily from the funeral home after the visitation last night. It is from Carla and Brad Meadows; I plan to put it in my office at the church. Sandra also gave each of us two plates of cake, leftover from the deserts that the church had brought. We took our two plates to Cindy's parents to share. We would spend the night with them, returning to High Point tomorrow.

Eventually, several of us began to make our way out with our items. I put our things in the car and then stood outside and talked with Sammy, Scott, Carol, Austin and Cindy. Sammy's dog, "Beaver," was also there; he has a kickball. Several of us kicked the ball and he would go and get it, dribbling it like a soccer player who has lots of energy. It was a mild and beautiful night.

I hugged them all goodbye and told each one that I loved them. I also reminded them how important it is that we stay in touch. I feel like everyone feels good about the family. We are as united as we have been for a long time. I have thought several times of the statement that Daddy had made that last Tuesday in November, "If it takes my death to bring my children together, then that makes me happy." I know that he is happy tonight.

Scott commented about the service today, "Everything went well. Daddy would be proud." Again, I was reminded of what Daddy had said several times, "God has worked everything out."

Yes, Daddy, He has.

We left around 9:10. As we drove down Sammy's long driveway, the moon was bright and the fields beautiful. We hoped to rest well tonight. I plan to return to High Point in the morning and will attempt to preach this Sunday. It will be hard to get back into the routine, but I will try, taking it one step at a time. I will surely give it my best effort. Daddy would do...and expect, no less.

CHAPTER 39

SATURDAY, JANUARY 15

A Time for Everything

As I hear the cuckoo clock strike, I am reminded of time, its blessings and its sorrows. I think about what the writer of Ecclesiastes said:

> *There is a time for everything,*
> *A season for every activity under*
> *heaven.*
> *A time to be born and a time to die.*
> *A time to plant and a time to*
> *harvest.*
> *A time to kill and a time to heal. (3:1-3a, NLT)*

The clock reminds me of the time that I received it as a gift. It carries me back to the spring of 2003. We had gone to Lumberton to get Daddy. We brought him back to Thomasville, and he stayed the weekend with us. It was the first and the last time that he came to our house here. He really enjoyed seeing what my life was all about.

When we took him back to his apartment that Sunday evening, Daddy had insisted on giving me something before we left. He had said, "I want to give you *something*." He was always the giver. He saw the clock, still in the box. It is a Black Forest Cuckoo Clock from Germany. He had a friend to pick it up for him when they had gone to Germany. It has hung on my wall in our living room ever since. I wind it daily. Now it reminds me of how precious…and fleeting, time is. Daddy had insisted that I take it. I did not know it then, but that clock is one of a handful of the most valuable possessions that I own. *He* gave it to me. But it reminds me of time…

I think about time, represented as dates on the calendar. Those dates are forever etched in my memory:

November 16, 2004—Daddy came to High Point to live at the nursing home.

November 28, 2004—Daddy was moved to *High Point Regional Hospital.*

December 9, 2004—Daddy was told that he had terminal lung cancer.

December 15, 2004—He came back to the nursing home, free of pneumonia, but gradually became consumed by cancer.

January 3, 2005—He died at a specific time, 2:00 p. m. He was with us in High Point for 49 days, seven weeks. He came on a Tuesday and died on a Monday.

January 6, 2005—I conducted his funeral at 11:00 a. m.

October 21—He was born in 1927; he would have been 78 this year. He died at age 77.

I'm reminded of the time that is *past…*

There are so many things that happened before all of this began that I remember. They are literally frozen in time, those times that I remember being with Daddy. Times of celebration and joy…
—*My graduation from college in South Carolina*: I have a picture of that event in my office. It's only a small picture, but it has

me in the middle, with Mama on my right and Daddy on my left. I was so proud to have them both there.

—*My graduation from seminary in Kentucky*: Daddy made the trip. We had a wonderful time afterwards.

—*The day that I got married*: Daddy was there. He was my best man, giving me his support and some last minute advice.

—*The day that I received my doctorate (D. Min.) in New Jersey*: *That* picture I have already spoken of in this account. I also remember the meal after the graduation. We had supper at a *very* ritzy restaurant. It was actually a train car, no longer in use. We laughed so hard, as only Daddy could laugh, that night. Sammy's stomach growled before the meal, making a very unusual sound. Daddy laughed that laugh where he would moan as he drew air back into his lungs. I've never laughed so hard...

It was also the night that he gave me $250 in cash before the meal, telling me to pay for it when they brought the check, but not mentioning that he had given me the money. He was always giving.

Thank you, Daddy, for that memory.

—*The times at White Lake*: The family went for several years. Daddy would rent the house and all of us children would buy the food. He loved to quietly sit on the pier, *sometimes* getting into the water. He would sleep late, catching up on some rest during the time away from the drug store. Then, the grandkids grew up and we all went our separate ways. But I remember...

—*The family gatherings*: We celebrated Thanksgivings at Carol's and Christmases at Sammy's. I remember Christmas last year. Daddy came by after supper had started. He was concerned about Uncle Frank and had come from his house. Uncle Frank was dying of cancer. He passed away on January 8, 2004. Little did we know that Daddy would follow him only 360 days later, less than one year.

It is funny how time comes and goes and things change.

Uncle R. C. died in May of 2003, Uncle Frank in January of 2004 and Daddy in January of 2005; three brothers, less than two years. I was anticipating Daddy coming to our house after his rehabilitation at the nursing home. I was hoping he could enjoy the clock that he had given us. Now, I know he never will.

—*The time we went to Italy, the mid 90s*: Daddy took Ashly and myself with him. We flew to Milan, then spent two nights in Venice, then on to Florence and finally Rome. I remember how much fun it was. I also remember the hot weather. I recall how odd Daddy was that first night, after being awake for such a long trip; he was disoriented. I was concerned for him, but attributed it to tiredness. Now I wonder if that was all that it was. We will never know.

The three of us went to Assisi. We saw the Basilica of Saint Francis. Weeks later, an earthquake would damage it forever. I bought a couple of small necklaces made from olive wood that day. They are shaped like the Greek letter "tau," or "T." Mama has worn that cross from the day I brought it to her. She said that she rubs it in times of trouble and it brings her peace. The other one has been in a box on my dresser...until I got back home from the funeral. I put it around my neck that day. I will wear it every day for the rest of my life. It brings me comfort to know that Mama wears one just like it. I also find comfort in that it came from a point in time that was one of the most pleasurable ones I've experienced up to this point in my life. It was time spent with my father.

It's funny how some things do not change.

That Franciscan cross reminds me that Daddy ultimately found the Savior who died on it. As we walked around all of that history in Italy, little could I have expected that Daddy would one day find the Savior that it referenced.

—*The times at the drug store in Lumberton*: Over the years, Cindy and I have been privileged to visit Daddy and David there. I have visited several times, but now wish I had visited just a few more. On one of those visits, before Daddy's first fall and before he was in his wheelchair or on the walker, he handed me his business card. It has the pharmacy emblem, along with his personal information and the phrase "Licensed over 50 years" on it. I brought it back to High Point and thought little of it. Now, I plan to have it matted and framed. It will hold a place of prominence in my office. Again, it represents a moment in time...*He* handed it to me...

I am reminded of the time that is *recent past...*

The last seven weeks with Daddy have seemed like seven months to me. I can hardly believe that it has only been seven *weeks*. At that time, Daddy came to High Point. It seems like months ago that I met him in his room, 108. The first words out of his mouth as he lay on his back in his room that day were, "Have I gone to heaven?" I remember telling him, "No, Daddy, you are in High Point." Now, however, you *are* in heaven.

He was very tired that day. He had traveled almost three hours by ambulance from Lumberton. Upon his arrival, he had said that the ambulance attendant commented, "Mr. Cavanaugh, you are not in Kansas anymore." He had chuckled as he told me about his trip. He had told them as they had passed through Ellerbe, "Turn around, I think you missed a bump." That was the first laugh that we shared in High Point; thankfully, it would not be our last.

While I remember a lot of things about Daddy, my strongest memories will always be of his time with us in High Point, memories of him in his bed, always in his bed. I remember his stay at the hospital, those times when he actually seemed to feel comfortable. He was alert, talkative and content. He was so pleased with the care that he had received. While he was there, he told me that he had noticed the plaques on the wall leading into 7 North. He later commented to me that he would like for us to put a plaque there sometime thanking them for his care. I ordered that plaque the first of this week. I plan to take it to the staff on 7 North when it is ready. I went by the hospital to tell them that it is coming. One of Daddy's nurses cried when I told her about his suffering that last morning of his life. Daddy had that effect on people, regardless of who they were or where he was; they always fell in love with his smile and pleasant personality. The plaque will hang on the wall Daddy noticed. It will read:

Given in recognition and appreciation of the care our father, Samuel MacDonald Cavanaugh, RPh., received by the staff of 7 North from 11/28/04-12/15/04. He was so comfortable during his time here. Given in his memory by his children: Sammy, David, Carol, Roland and Scott. As Daddy would say, "But the best of all is, God is with us."

I remember those days in the nursing home as well; his days in High Point are not all bad memories for me. Most of that time he was able to talk and laugh in spite of the pain. I remember preparing his teeth for him so he could eat, until he stopped wearing them. I remember helping him to get settled on so many nights, adjusting his TV or lights. Sometimes I would lower him down so he could rest. Even though they are memories of a man on his back, they are memories of a man who had found peace, as Daddy himself testified to several times. I remember his saying, more than once, that a lot of people could not understand the peace he had found, or so he felt. I told him that was true, but also reminded him that many people have found, and do find, that peace that comes from God's grace alone. He had found that grace and its resultant peace.

The father I came to know, *really* know those 49 days, was the caring one. It was not the one who both disappointed and was disappointed in this life. He was finally able to let himself go while he was here. He was able to make things right with his family...and with God. I didn't see his problems or the things he had done in the past, but rather the man that he became through the process of dying. He was not only dying physically, but he had died to himself, along with the regrets and pains associated with the "old man." He became a "new creation" through God's grace. It was the man that he was all along; but it was only as he was wasting away that that man was able to finally emerge. As C. S. Lewis said of finding out about his wife's cancer, "It is incredible how much happiness, how much joy we sometimes had together after all hope was gone." I love the man that my daddy was; but most of all I love the man that he ultimately became. But that man, the one that I really came to know, is gone now. However, I like what Barbara Johnson has said, "I like to think of my dad as not gone, but just gone on ahead." Daddy has gone on ahead. Without coming to High Point, he may never have prepared himself or us for his departure. God's grace is truly amazing.

When a person dies, we sometimes have selfish thoughts. Not long after Daddy died, I was already thinking, "What will I do with the time I've spent with him, all of those hours and days?" I was there every day he was in High Point but one. Most days, I was there for lunch and supper. I began asking myself, "What will I do with that time? How will I deal with the memory of how that time has been filled?"

Then the events surrounding the funeral hit me. I was so concerned with being strong for my family that I soon forgot the questions that I had been asking. It was only on returning home from his funeral that the weight of what had happened returned to me. I remember bringing in all of our "stuff," then falling into Cindy's arms, asking her, "Is it okay if I cry now?" I cried and cried. Later that night, I began going through some of the items I have that belonged to Daddy. When I began looking through his wallet, the emotions returned again. I knelt behind the couch and cried; then I cried some more. After the final sympathy card arrives, I will put all of his belongings away until I am ready to look through them. It may be six months; it may be two years. It is still too painful. It has only been 12 days. I thought I was "turning the corner" yesterday; I did not cry. Tonight, however, the swell of emotions has surfaced yet again. I know that it will get better. At the visitation someone told me that the pain eventually subsides, but the good memories stay forever. I welcome that time.

For now, though, the cards that came to the nursing home after Daddy's death will remain unopened. They are addressed to him, not me. He is not here to open them. I will not open them either...

I am reminded of the time that is *present*...

We removed the birdfeeders from outside of Daddy's window on the day that he died. One is on my window by the kitchen table. The other joins the feeders that we already had in our yard. The birds remind me of life. Even in the cold of winter life goes on. In the winter of Daddy's life, the birds still came. Even as his eyes slowly grew dim, he could still see the birds outside of his window. It was one of the few pleasures that a dying man might enjoy. Those feeders will forever remind me that even in death, Daddy has actually flown away. He flew away into God's arms. We can fly there too.

Just as Daddy slowly let go of this life, we too must let go. He left in a moment, on the wings of an angel. We may need more time to let go of him.

While the tears still come, the pain has already begun to subside. While at times when I least expect it, I may become upset, the overwhelming sense of loss is beginning to be interwoven into the everyday fabric of life. He will always be missed. But I must remember that just as Daddy's illness came to a conclusion over time, so the grieving process will come to a conclusion, or at least be more developed than it is at this present time, eventually. But it will take time.

There are a couple of thoughts that will sustain me in the days to come. The first thought is of God's nearness. As Daddy loved to say, "But the best of all is, God is with us." How true that statement is. Daddy knows its truth in an even greater way than we do at this time. But I know that it is true; He *is* with us.

The final thought has to do with eternal existence. Once again I remember Daddy's statement, "I want to remain as alert as I can, for as long as I can." That, and pain management, were his two major concerns the last few weeks that he lived here. His death brought an end to his pain, and now, I know that he is more alert than he has ever been.

How long can you remain alert, Daddy?

For as long as God Himself exists.

How long is that?

Forever.

CHAPTER 40

TUESDAY, JANUARY 25

How Long Will I Count the Days?

B efore I got out of bed this morning, I cried. Cindy and I have come to Holden Beach for some "down time." I went back into the office for the entire week last week, but was anticipating this time away. Cindy and I are not calling it a vacation, but rather "time away." After going home to Wallace Friday, we came to the beach on Sunday evening. There is a couple from our church that has a condo here. It is on the second floor with a direct view of the ocean. I can see the waves now. It is a beautiful day, and the sun is reflecting off of the water. Odie is stretched out by the balcony door, warming in the sun. Cindy and I were here this past July. Little did we know then that our lives would be changing in such a dramatic fashion. At that time the weather was warm; this trip has been very cold.

I miss him so much. I had not really cried since this past Saturday. I went by the grave for the first time since the day of the funeral, alone. As I drove around to where he is buried, I told myself that I was not going to cry. As I got out of the car, however, the tears began to flow. I found myself talking to him again, telling him how sorry I am that we missed so many years of spending time together. In a way, I feel that I am responsible for lost time as much as he is. After all, couldn't I have gone to *him* when I became an adult? I visited him some. At that time, I was the one who was too busy. I was busy getting an education, trying to help others, but neglecting the opportunity to spend time with my father. Now...that opportunity is gone forever. I thank God for those weeks that we had together. I realize that all things worked out just as they should have. That is what Daddy had said...he is probably right.

But today, am I crying for my own seeming neglect, or the loss of Daddy in death? I'm not sure, but feel confident that it is probably some of both. God's grace, however, rises to the forefront of my mind. Daddy could have died in his apartment alone. He could have coughed up blood. He could have never told the stories that he was able to tell during those seven weeks that we had together. He could have *not* had the opportunity to tell *us* the things that he needed to tell. He could *not* have had the opportunity to hear the things that we needed to tell *him*. He could have suffered so much more.

It has been over three weeks since he left us, three hours shy of 22 days. In a way it seems longer than the entire time that he was in High Point. I wonder how long will I count the days? How long will I cry for him? How many days will pass before I do not cry for him any longer? How many days will pass before I do not feel sadness when I think of him? Maybe there will always be a tinge of pain when I think of *him*, *his* suffering, *his* cancer, *his* pain. I'm not sure...

Today, though, he is walking. He is running and maybe even dancing. He may be exploring history, the history of the universe itself. I'm convinced that heaven is the ultimate history lover's dream come true. Anything that he wants to know is now known. Any question he has ever had is now answered. And he has cried his last tear.

"God, help those of us who remain to accept your comfort and peace as well. While we have questions about life...and suffering, give us the grace to live in that tension, for now. Remind us that we too will one day have all of these questions answered. One day, may we be fully alert...forever. Amen."

Revelation 21 contains the words, "He will remove all of their sorrows, and there will be no more death or sorrow or crying or pain. For the old world and its evils are gone forever!" (21:4, NLT).

Therein lies my comfort...and my hope.

ACT 4
FEBRUARY

WRITING A NEW STORY

The unexamined life is not worth living for man.

—Socrates

CHAPTER 41

WEDNESDAY, FEBRUARY 2
Further Down the Road

I went to talk with the *Hospice* bereavement counselor yesterday. She had called and asked me if I wanted to come by for a visit; I didn't hesitate to make the appointment. We met in her office at 1:00. She asked me to take any pictures of Daddy that I might have. I took a couple from my office, one with Daddy, Mama and me at my college graduation, and the Drew University picture that I have described in this journal.

The meeting was beneficial, I think. She asked me if had been angry? I have. Had I been apathetic? I have. Does almost everything seem trivial? It does. Do I feel like I don't want to be bothered by others? I do. She told me that I was circumstantially depressed. She offered to prescribe some short-term medication, but I declined. She said that it was better if I could get through this un-medicated. As sad as I sometimes feel, I want to experience all of the emotions involved. I remember when Mama's second husband, Hoover, died. She was so distraught; Daddy had given her something to take during that time. She doesn't remember very much about the funeral and said later that she didn't like the feeling. The counselor told me to give myself six months, at least; tomorrow is one month. While I am not overwhelmed with sadness very often, I am a bit down, along with all of the other symptoms she asked me about to open our session.

"The journal is very healthy," she said. She gave me some starting points for journaling ideas. She especially mentioned writing a letter to Daddy. She informed me that it was very hard to write a letter to a dead person, emotionally speaking, but very therapeutic. I plan to write him a letter in this journal, eventually...

As our session ended, she told me that we could meet again, or either I could participate in group counseling. The group is for those who have lost a parent or spouse; it is actually a support group. The first session is February 21st and it will meet several Mondays from 5:30-7:00. I told her I would like to meet with the group. Although I have actually had limited training in grief and its stages, I know that I need to share what I am going through and what I am feeling with those who have gone through a similar experience. I will regret it if I do not take the opportunity being offered to me. Maybe the sessions are the answer I have been looking for over these last few weeks. I am confident that I will benefit from them.

As I look back, I thought I was more prepared for Daddy to die. He and I had even talked about having time for *both* of us to prepare for his impending death. While I had remarked on one occasion that although I could never prepare fully, I could be "further down the road;" I now see the vanity of such a statement. One can try to prepare for death all that one wants, but the finality of it is beyond all attempts at preparation.

Time will eventually help me to sort things out in my life; I know that. However, until that time comes, I will need to take advantage of every opportunity to get me through this grieving process. It is a process.

I must give this process time...

CHAPTER 42

FRIDAY, FEBRUARY 18

I Love the Sun

After six weeks, the strongest sting of Daddy's death has passed, but I'm not fooling myself. I know that when I go to the bereavement support group this Monday, it will all come rushing back at me. I haven't really cried in a couple of weeks, but have had times when I probably could have. I'm not so naive as to think that I am "over it." As Lewis Grizzard said of his own father's death, "You never stop loving your Daddy." I now know exactly what he means.

For now, though, I must begin to bring this journal to a conclusion, if that is possible. I'm sure that I will write other entries about Daddy. But I want to, need to, start the process of bringing this one to some type of closure. I have written every word by hand in this worn, black book for over ten weeks now, every page a testament to my father. My struggle to "come to terms" with his suffering and death, and the evidence of God's goodness, are manifested in every one of its 176 hand-written pages. But, just as I have completed other things relative to Daddy's death, I now want to complete this "formal" record of my father's life, death and thoughts related to each. It has not been easy, but it has been the most significant thing that I have ever written. I'm not sure if it "will be of interest" to anyone else, as Daddy said it might, but it has certainly benefited me. I also have a strong suspicion that he benefited from the knowledge that I was recording his daily routine, struggles, stories, dreams, fears and hopes. He told me on one occasion that he wished he had made a record of his father's life. While this has not been a record of my father's entire life, it is a record of "life," the one that he came to know those last seven weeks of his earthly existence. It was a life filled with pain and suffering, but also laughter, joy, numerous visits and phone calls, cards, prayers and sacred moments with his children. It is a life that lives on after his death…in my memory.

There is an image that comes to mind of him that I do not want to forget. It is an image, yet unrecorded within these pages, of contentment and uncluttered, innocent pleasure. It is an image that I will always cherish…

* * *

It was November 21st, a Sunday. Daddy had been at the nursing home for almost five days. I went by to see him after church and found him in his gerry chair. As we visited, he finished his lunch. Around 2:00 one of the physical therapists came by to introduce herself and to see if he felt up to some initial physical therapy. Her name was Kelly Shannon, from Pennsylvania. Upon hearing her name, Daddy immediately began to talk to her about Ireland. He had visited that country a couple of times, so he inquired as to her background. Her father's father was from Ireland, though she had never been. Daddy began to tell her about how beautiful the country was. He told her about kissing the "blarney stone" for good luck; he had actually done so. He was always so proud of our family's Irish heritage. (Our ancestors are from County Cavan, Ireland.) After more "small talk," she asked him if he felt up to some physical therapy; he said that he did. (He never turned down an opportunity to perhaps help himself to walk again.) She then asked him if he would like to go outside; the weather was nice for that time of year. He was delighted at the possibility.

She took him from his room to the patio adjacent to the TV room on his hall. I remember that it was a beautiful day. The sun was brightly shining, though there was a light breeze. She turned him in his chair, towards the sun. He was facing the street near the patio, wearing a sweatshirt and sweat pants, and seemed to be very comfortable.

Having situated him, the sun being in his face, he squinted. She asked him if he wanted her to move him to where the sun would not be in his face. His exact words were, "No, I love the sun." He smiled a big smile and looked as happy as I have ever seen him. After five days in his room, he was obviously overjoyed to be outside. I remember that the session was virtually non-productive. His legs twitched from the knee down, much like a reflex when struck with a doctor's hammer. That was probably the last time he had any movement below his waist, and he worked very hard that day to achieve one repetition with each leg, one *very small* repetition. But he was in the sun, and he was thrilled...

* * *

When Cindy and I went to Holden beach a few weeks ago, we explored several thrift stores. Some people go to yard sales; we go to thrift stores. At one of the stores we walked through, I found a personal treasure. We were at a store in Calabash when I saw it hanging on the back wall in the rear of the business. As soon as I saw it, I knew that it was worth the ten dollars that the shop owner was asking for it. It is a multi-colored print, with calligraphy. It is dated "1961" and in a beautiful wooden frame. The words are from a famous verse that I had heard Daddy quote from years ago. He did not mention it while he was with us in High Point, but I remember him quoting it word for word in days gone by.

It speaks of many things. As I read it, I am reminded of him in several ways. A couple of characteristics of that verse stand out:

It speaks of sunshine, warm on the face...
It speaks of Ireland...
It speaks of God holding us in the palm of His hand, just like the song from Daddy's funeral...

That print, with its Celtic, multi-colored border, hangs in my den over several pictures that we have displayed on a table. Among the pictures are three that are close to my heart:

The picture of Daddy and me in Carol's den; she gave it to me after the visitation at the funeral home that night.
The picture of Daddy on the boat in Greece, the sun on his face...and
The picture of Daddy and us kids at Christmas at Sammy's in 1996. (It was the first picture that we displayed in his room at the nursing home; I had placed it on his TV.)

The print also hangs just below the cuckoo clock that Daddy gave us almost two years ago now.

I believe that God led me to the print as a way of His comfort, right when I needed it most. My prayer is that the verse will settle on my mind and rest in my heart, until we meet again...

The title of the verse is *An Irish Blessing*. It reads:

May the road rise to meet you.
May the wind always be at your back.
May the sun shine warm upon your face,
the rains fall soft upon your fields and,
until we meet again,
May God hold you in the palm of his hand.

I can only add, may that blessing be ours.

CHAPTER 43

MONDAY, FEBRUARY 21

A Familiar Lump

I have performed two funerals since Daddy's death. I did the funeral for Iola Eudy on February 4th. I actually played a minor role while O. W. Willis helped and James Smith had the major part of the service. Having two other ministers to help me made it easier. But yesterday, I did my first funeral…solo.

Nancy and her husband are members of the care group that Cindy and I attend. Her mother would have been 100 in June; she died this past Thursday. She had been in a nursing facility. While I know Nancy and her husband, I had never seen or met Mrs. Pratt.

The funeral went okay, but as I preceded the casket to the grave, I felt that familiar lump coming up in my throat. It is a feeling that I have been able to squelch over the last several weeks. While I did not lose control at the graveside, I could not prevent my eyes from becoming moist with tears. After the graveside service was concluded, I walked over to the side of the tent and allowed a few tears to flow, trying desperately to not let anyone see. Naomi, from our care group as well, noticed. She said, "It has not been very long, has it?" I responded, "No, but I will be all right." After a moment, I was fine. Not fine, but I was okay to go back to my car.

I didn't really think about it much more yesterday, but I had that same feeling again this morning. It has been with me throughout this first part of the day. I realize that Daddy was almost my age when he lost his father. Did he have the same struggles that I am having? I guess my mind also goes back to the realization that Daddy died seven weeks ago today, at 2:00, the exact length of time that he was with us in High Point. He *lived* here for 49 days; he has *been gone* for 49 days.

Also, today is the first of five bereavement group meetings at *Hospice*. While I look forward to the outlet, I'm not sure that I look forward to resurrecting all of those memories and emotions yet again. But I know that it will be helpful. I know that I will benefit from it and I have even made the comment that I want to get whatever I can that will help me. I have read two books, one on losing a parent, the other on grieving the loss of a father. I have yet another one, given to me by Jonathan Lewis, *Confessions of a Grieving Christian* by Zig Zigler. While it is typically not my natural interest in reading material, I find myself devouring everything that I find or am given on the subject.

So, I'm not exactly sure what will happen at the meeting tonight, but I am going with an open mind and heart. It is helpful to know that I am not alone, to know there are others that I can talk with who are traveling this same road.

"God, help me to be what I should be during this time. Help me to think of others who are suffering similar loss, and not myself only. Amen."

CHAPTER 44

SUNDAY, FEBRUARY 27

He Was Walking

I dreamed about Daddy this morning. I awoke from sleep very early; it was 2:45. I awoke after his visit today.

The *Hospice* bereavement counselor had said at our last meeting that it was unusual for a person to dream about someone who is close to you once they die; it is not unheard of, however. I don't really know if I was desiring to dream about him or not. Nevertheless, this morning, my father came to me.

I was in a place with a lot of other people. We were all rather busy, but I'm not exactly sure what it was that we were doing. It's hard to explain the context of some dreams; this dream was like that. We were in a place, much like a gathering for a meeting. I don't know where *I was*, but I certainly know how *I felt*...

I was not a "slave," but could sense that I had been given a heavy responsibility. The responsibility was what a servant might feel obligated to do. All I know is that it was overwhelming. I could sense a heaviness of heart and a loss of direction. I'm sure I was there not out of desire, but out of compulsion. I was there with lots of other people who evidently felt the same way, or at least were in a similar, depressing situation.

We were allowed to write letters seeking help for our situation, whatever it was. Again, the details of my occupation are not clear, but the way I felt is very concise: I was depressed and overwhelmed, as if there was no one there to help. I wrote some letters; I'm not sure to whom I wrote them, but they were written to several people. I do know that Daddy was one of them. I needed his help desperately. I needed to hear from him. I needed him to come to me. The letters got to the various people, I could tell, including the one to Daddy.

At some point, hearing a commotion, we all ceased our work; someone was coming. I could sense that it was one of the recipients of a letter, mine, or someone else's I could not tell. All eyes were turned towards what was apparently the door. The person was coming into view. I sensed that I knew who it was. Could it be? And then I saw him...

It was my father. He was coming into the large room where we were gathered. He was greeting everyone in the crowd. It was almost like a scene from a movie, where the victorious hero has finally returned home safe and sound. He was *walking* and smiling, and shaking hands with everyone in the room. They all clamored to reach him as he came further into that place. He hugged some. I could tell that they all knew him. It was obvious that they loved him immensely. He was very pleased and enjoying the scene more than I can explain. He knew all of them as well. I did not recognize any face, except his.

After what seemed an eternity, he finally began moving my way. My heart skipped a beat. As he turned towards me, he walked more quickly. He came and stood in front of me. I could hardly contain the emotion swelling up within me. I was thinking that I could not wait to fall into his arms...

As I looked into his eyes, those deep blue eyes, he smiled the smile that only he could smile. He tilted his head to the side, as if to say, "Come to me." I could not contain myself as I reached out to his open arms and fell into them. I held him and he held me. My only response was open weeping. I cried and I cried, much like the day I fell into Cindy's arms after the funeral was finished, and we had returned home.

As we embraced, he finally spoke. He shared the same words over and over, "Roland, it's all right. Everything is all right." As we held each other, the image began to fade to black, as if on cue...

As my eyes opened, I could tell that it was a dream. The sounds of the house in the small hours of the morning returned, Cindy breathing softly by my side, the clock ticking and the dog yawning. I was not crying as the dream concluded, but tears began to flow as I realized that Daddy had visited me one more time to reassure me that "Everything is all right." He knew that I needed to hear from him; God knew it as well.

For the first time in many weeks, I feel that I have visited with him once again. While I cannot get to him at this time, *perhaps* he has come to me. No, he *has* come to me. Any questions that I have, or any struggles related to his death, are put to rest. Finally, I have the assurance that I can go on with life. I know that he is encouraging me on this path. My mind goes to Hebrews 12. My father is even now cheering me on in my struggle. I will make it. We all will make it.

Everything *is* all right.

ACT 5
EPILOGUE

HOPE SPRINGS ETERNAL

Spring is a true reconstructionist.

—Henry Timrod

Tomorrow is the first day of spring.

I am alone for the next few days as Cindy visits her parents. She was hesitant to leave me alone. It is the first time that I have been by myself since she last visited them for a few days following Thanksgiving. I assured her that I would be fine. As I returned to the house, however, I began to wonder if it is too early. I have thought about him today more than at any time in recent memory. Though I think of him every day, almost every moment, today has been different.

Carol and Mike visited us for several days this week. While she visited with Cindy during the day, Mike and I both headed to our respective places of employment, his in Raleigh, and mine in High Point. We were together at night though, and it was nice to have the company. Carol continues to work out her grief in her own way, as we all do I suppose. But yesterday, Mike went to work and Carol went home. Cindy and I met her parents for lunch in Dunn, about three hours from here; she went on with them. Perhaps the pleasure of all of us being together makes my loneliness a little more pronounced. Regardless, I am now officially alone...

I wonder if he ever felt like that? I know that family surrounded him during those last days, not to mention several friends, some from nearby, others coming from considerable distances. Still, when you are looking death straight in the eye, does all of that company lessen the loneliness? It's just you and death surrounded by the living. I would love to ask him how it felt in those final days...those final hours...those final minutes. I can't help but think that the family and friends at hand somehow made his passing from this world to the next a bit easier to handle. At least, I want with all of my heart to think that is the case. Daddy was not alone; I know that. But did our presence carry him over with confidence? He seemed to be at peace. He spoke about feeling peaceful. But how does it all play out when death finally taps your shoulder and says that it is time to go, time to leave the familiar, the family, the friends, the sounds, the smells and the sights? Daddy, how did it feel?

* * *

As spring is the time of *life*, the time of *new things*, I thought it appropriate to plant a tree. The tree was a gift from our care group, the one that Cindy and I attend on a weekly basis. It was bought with a gift certificate given to me by the group. The members of the group had gotten it from a local nursery here in Thomasville. They had suggested in the card that I plant a tree in memory of Daddy. At that time, I felt like it was a wonderful idea; I still do. So I decided, with Cindy's help, to buy a flowering crabapple. The blossoms are the color of wine, a deep burgundy, simply beautiful. Since I was alone today, I took a few minutes to plant the tree in my front yard in memory of my daddy. It is near the bird feeder brought from the nursing home, the one that stood on the pole outside of his window. Now, of course, the feeder stands right outside of my front window near his tree.

As I dug the hole, I cried. As I mixed the peat with the soil, I cried. And as I watered it, my tears mixed with those droplets of water that will give it nourishment. It is almost as if my spirit was nourished as my tears flowed in a way not dissimilar to the nourishment those droplets of water give to the tree. Tears truly are good for the soul.

I have decided to call my tree "Sam." It seems the most obvious choice for a name. I pray that it lives. I pray hard that it lives...

Daddy would be pleased. He liked plants. At times, he would even keep several in the house in Whiteville, under a very large fluorescent light fixture. I think he would be pleased with my choice of the type of tree also, for it points to life; life that I am convinced he found in death. In a way, life was never as full for him as it could have been, no, *should* have been. While he gave himself to so many, he struggled for years with his own personal demons. His life was defined by giving to others, but I'm afraid that his shortcomings and struggles kept him from having the fullness of life that he really deserved. We all deserve it. However, each spring, when the crabapple blooms, I will be reminded that he did find life's fullness...in death.

* * *

The birds are now coming to his feeder, by his tree, in earnest. I saw several today as I went about the task of planting it. There were cardinals, titmice, cowbirds and sparrows. I also saw several doves gathering seeds from the ground at the base of the feeder. Birds and trees will forever remind me of him. While I don't know when, I look forward to the day when the birds will make their way from the feeder to the tree, *Daddy's tree.*

And when the crabapple blooms, and the birds fill its branches, I will know that life is indeed going on as it has for ages past. The thought makes me feel better somehow. My prayer is that God will nourish us and provide a place for us to finally come to rest as well, much like the birds in the crabapple tree. I know that just as that tree extends its branches invitingly to the birds, so God extends His arms out to all of us. He will give us food for our tears and His strong arms for our support.

Live on, Sam. That is my sincere prayer.

When the Crabapple Blooms

By Roland E. Cavanaugh

When the crabapple blooms, I will remember you,
remember the pain that you felt.
When its dark blooms appear, my thoughts turn to you,
thoughts of suffering that make my heart melt.

The plant was a gift from good, loving friends,
who stood close at hand in my pain.
In their kind, loving words, they suggested to me,
that this tree would live on in your name.

When the crabapple blooms, I will remember you,
remember the pain that you felt.
When its dark blooms appear, my thoughts turn to you,
thoughts of suffering that make my heart melt.

The day it was planted, by the strength of my hand,
I watered it freely with tears.
As each drop of sorrow fell onto its roots,
my heart was relieved of its fears.

When the crabapple blooms, I will remember you,
remember the pain that you felt.
When its dark blooms appear, my thoughts turn to you,
thoughts of suffering that make my heart melt.

The prayer that I prayed, as I covered that mound,
was that the young sapling might live.
I still cry out to God, in a daily report,
"May it have all of the strength You can give."

When the crabapple blooms, I will remember you,
remember the pain that you felt.
When its dark blooms appear, my thoughts turn to you,
thoughts of suffering that make my heart melt.

While the blooms they remind me that things go on living,
and that life yet comes through when we die.
Still their pedals bring sadness and cause me to ponder,
the reason for the tears that I cry.

When the crabapple blooms, I will remember you,
remember the pain that you felt.
When its dark blooms appear, my thoughts turn to you,
thoughts of suffering that make my heart melt.

The flowers bring beauty to the eye of the beholder,
the fruit provides food for the birds.
The branches give shelter from the threatening weather,
and offer comfort like well-spoken words.

When the crabapple blooms, I will remember you,
remember the pain that you felt.
When its dark blooms appear, my thoughts turn to you,
thoughts of suffering that make my heart melt.

As the crabapple grows, gaining strength and endurance,
a symbol of health it will be.
When the birds leave its branches, and soar to the heavens,
it reminds me that you are now free.

When the crabapple blooms, I will remember you,
remember the pain that you felt.
When its dark blooms appear, my thoughts turn to you,
thoughts of suffering that make my heart melt.

April 4, 2005

Funeral and Graveside Scriptures

Opening Scripture: 2 Corinthians 4:7-5:9 (NLT)

7But this precious treasure—this light and power that now shine within us—is held in perishable containers, that is, in our weak bodies. So everyone can see that our glorious power is from God and is not our own. 8We are pressed on every side by troubles, but we are not crushed and broken. We are perplexed, but we don't give up and quit. 9We are hunted down, but God never abandons us. We get knocked down, but we get up again and keep going. 10Through suffering, these bodies of ours constantly share in the death of Jesus so that the life of Jesus may also be seen in our bodies. 11Yes, we live under constant danger of death because we serve Jesus, so that the life of Jesus will be obvious in our dying bodies. 12So we live in the face of death, but it has resulted in eternal life for you. 13But we continue to preach because we have the same kind of faith the psalmist had when he said, "I believed in God, and so I speak." 14We know that the same God who raised our Lord Jesus will also raise us with Jesus and present us to himself along with you. 15All of these things are for your benefit. And as God's grace brings more and more people to Christ, there will be great thanksgiving, and God will receive more and more glory. 16That is why we never give up. Though our bodies are dying, our spirits are being renewed every day. 17For our present troubles are quite small and won't last very long. Yet they produce for us an immeasurably great glory that will last forever! [18]*So we don't look at the troubles we can see right now; rather, we look forward to what we have not yet seen. For the troubles we see will soon be over, but the joys to come will last forever.* [1]*For we know that when this earthly tent we live in is taken down—when we die and leave these bodies—we will have a home in heaven, an eternal body made for us by God himself and not by human hands.* [2]*We grow weary in our present bodies, and we long for the day when we will put on our heavenly bodies like new clothing.* [3]*For we will not be spirits without bodies, but we will put on new heavenly bodies.* [4]*Our dying bodies make us groan and sigh, but it's not that we want to die and have no bodies at all. We want to slip into our new bodies so that these dying bodies will be swallowed up by everlasting life.* [5]*God himself has prepared us for this, and as a guarantee he has given us his Holy Spirit.* [6]*So we are always confident, even though we know that as long as we live in these bodies we are not at home with the Lord.* [7]*That is why we live by believing and not by seeing.* [8]*Yes, we are fully confident, and we would rather be away from these bodies, for then we will be at home with the Lord.* [9]*So our aim is to please him always, whether we are here in this body or away from this body.*

Scripture used with the message: Ephesians 2:1-10 (NIV)

[1]*As for you, you were dead in your transgressions and sins,* [2]*in which you used to live when you followed the ways of this world and of the ruler of the kingdom of the air, the spirit who is now at work in those who are disobedient.* [3]*All of us also lived among them at one time, gratifying the cravings of our sinful nature and following its desires and thoughts. Like the rest, we were by nature objects of wrath.* [4]*But because of his great love for us, God, who is rich in mercy,* [5]*made us alive with Christ even when we were dead in transgressions—it is by grace you have been saved.* [6]*And God raised us up with Christ and seated us with him in the heavenly realms in Christ Jesus,* [7]*in order that in the coming ages he might show the incomparable riches of his grace, expressed in his kindness to us in*

Christ Jesus. [8]For it is by grace you have been saved, through faith—and this not from yourselves, it is the gift of God—[9]not by works, so that no one can boast. [10]For we are God's workmanship, created in Christ Jesus to do good works, which God prepared in advance for us to do.

<u>Scripture used at the graveside</u>: Revelation 21:1-7 (NKJV)

[1]Now I saw a new heaven and a new earth, for the first heaven and the first earth had passed away. Also there was no more sea. [2]Then I, John, saw the holy city, New Jerusalem, coming down out of heaven from God, prepared as a bride adorned for her husband. [3]And I heard a loud voice from heaven saying, "Behold, the tabernacle of God is with men, and He will dwell with them, and they shall be His people. God Himself will be with them and be their God. [4]And God will wipe away every tear from their eyes; there shall be no more death, nor sorrow, nor crying. There shall be no more pain, for the former things have passed away." [5]Then He who sat on the throne said, "Behold, I make all things new." And He said to me, "Write, for these words are true and faithful." [6]And He said to me, "It is done! I am the Alpha and the Omega, the Beginning and the End. I will give of the fountain of the water of life freely to him who thirsts. [7]He who overcomes shall inherit all things, and I will be his God and he shall be My son."

Recommended Resources

A Grief Observed by C. S. Lewis

A Time to Grieve by Carol Staudacher

Companion through the Darkness: Inner Dialogues on Grief
by Stephanie Ericsson

Confessions of a Grieving Christian by Zig Zigler

Good Grief by Granger E. Westberg

Healing After Loss by Martha Whitmore Hickman

How to Go on Living when Someone You Love Dies
by Therese A. Rondo

On Grieving the Death of a Father by Harold Ivan Smith

*Orphaned Adult: Understanding and Coping with Grief and
Change after the Death of Our Parents* by Alexander Levy

Name All the Animals: A Memoir by Alison Smith

Tracks of a Fellow Struggler: How to Handle Grief
    by John R. Claypool

Tuesdays with Morrie by Mitch Album

Understanding Grief: Helping Yourself Heal by Alan D. Wolfelt

When Grief is Your Constant Companion by Carolyn Rhea

When Your Parent Dies by Ron Klung

> *Well Daddy, it's finished.*
> "See you soon…"

Printed in the United States
44486LVS00004BA/15

9 781597 816519